Jelly Roll

To Mary Jo With
Personal Best Wishes,
Charlie Thomas

Jelly Roll

A Black Neighborhood in a Southern Mill Town

CHARLES E. THOMAS

The University of Arkansas Press
Fayetteville

ISBN-10: 1-55728-982-4
ISBN-13: 978-1-55728-982-7

16 15 14 13 12 5 4 3 2 1

♾ The paper used in this publication meets the minimum requirements of the American National Standard for Permanence of Paper for Printed Library Materials Z39.48-1984.

LIBRARY OF CONGRESS CATALOGING-IN-PUBLICATION DATA

Thomas, Charles E.
Jelly roll : a black neighborhood in a southern mill town / Charles E. Thomas.
p. cm.
Originally published: 1986. With new pref.
Includes bibliographical references.
ISBN 978-1-55728-982-7 (pbk. : alk. paper) — ISBN 1-55728-982-4 (pbk. : alk. paper)
1. African Americans—Arkansas—Calion--Social conditions. 2. African Americans—Arkansas—Calion—Economic conditions. 3. Calion (Ark.)—Social conditions. 4. Calion (Ark.)—Economic conditions. I. Title.
F419.C54T46 2012
305.896'073076761—dc23

2012005191

To my mentor
and
long-time friend,
John W. Bennett

Contents

Preface

The centerpiece of this book is a reissue, a third publication of my 1986 study: *Jelly Roll: A Black Neighborhood in a Southern Mill Town*, heretofore out of print but still in demand for its explicit historical narratives that mirror life's challenges.

Added in postscript are later interviews revealing attitudes of growing restlessness and dissatisfaction with the perceived slow movement toward racial equality and opportunity.

I, the author and sole researcher, am a white male—both a professional anthropologist who taught for seventeen years at Washington University in St. Louis, Missouri, and the operator of Calion Lumber Company in south Arkansas where this study was conducted.

My dual role in this study and in this community remains unchanged through these years and is set forth in the original introduction to *Jelly Roll*, which follows.

CHAPTER 1

History, Methodology, and Bias: a background to research in the black community of Calion, Arkansas.

This is an account of how Blacks live and think in the small (population 638) sawmill town of Calion in the piney woods of South Arkansas. Eighty-four black households comprise the study group and live together in a compact area consisting of two long blocks at right angles to each other near the entrance to the sawmill. This black neighborhood, with its distinct boundaries and close living quarters within the town proper, has long been called Jelly Roll. Our book is concerned solely with the black people of this neighborhood community and their changing character over three living generations.

Interviewing one or more members of some seventy percent of the black households in Calion, I conducted this study working alone over a three-year period. Although I am a professionally trained anthropologist who spent over fifteen years in teaching and research at Washington University in St. Louis, I am also the proprietor of the sawmill at Calion. I began this study fully aware of the contradictions and ambiguities involved in such an effort. I am white. The study community is all black. What chance do I have to develop a meaningful and candid rapport with black mill workers and their families under these circumstances? Will thirty years of mutual acquaintance and good personal relations compensate at least in part for these differences? To what degree can I view the community objectively as a kind of insider, which I am, but also as an outsider and observer? When describing the past sorrows of black poverty, do I not bring blame to my own doorstep? Although I resist the accusation of exploitation of the poor, still I must confess that through the years I have felt a growing awareness that I could have been a more generous employer.

But self-recrimination hangs in a web of extenuating circumstances, never firm, but rather based upon memories comprising innumerable individual decisions made over the years. Throughout my long tenure in the mill's management, I have consistently behaved as an avid entrepreneur, committed to the capitalist system, believing deeply that, despite its obvious imperfections and sometimes gross inequities, it remains man's best means of sustenance and survival. By taking shelter within the mercantile system in which our sawmill and its community is a microcosm, I must emphasize the dominance of an unyielding raw commodity market to which all lumber manufacturers must adhere. Today in an era of mergers and massive conglomerates, even the largest lumber company commands less than ten percent of the market. Such market conditions,typified by sharp price fluctuations and competition in a labor-intensive industry, have afforded narrow margins for rendering social justice. Therefore, for better or for worse, the social implications of our management of the enterprise are a judgement left to you, the reader, as this volume unfolds.

My fifteen years among the "theory class" in a large academic department in the social sciences have served to aggravate my natural distrust of the abstract. The dual role that I played through the years as a capitalist-academic has given me good peripheral vision if nothing else, and has made me specially skeptical of calls for purity of research and professional objectivity. Without subjecting the general reader to the academic arguments, I will simply state that I have long since rejected most social science aspirations to total neutrality or objectivity as self-deluding, pseudoscientific by nature, and sterile in their commission. By and large these purist productions lie unread on the back shelves of academe. Moreover, we glimpse the backside of objectivity via a researcher's various connections with money and power: foundation grants and fellowships, "good old boy" associations, graduate student fiefdoms, academic clout and territoriality. In short, it is obvious that the goods and services that comprise the academic machine were not produced in an ethically pure or value free milieu.

My own models in cultural anthropology are, on the whole, the popular, well-published scholars in the field. They include Margaret Mead, Ruth Benedict, Collin Turnbull, Oscar Lewis and

Herbert Gans, all of whom shared a sensitivity to good editorial journalism, factual reporting through their own eyes, and a sanguine involvement with their subjects. Art, not science, prevails in their best works.

A brief vignette of my own involvement with the community to be studied is in order. My family were all native St. Louisans. It was my grandfather Thomas, who in 1916 got wind of a good deal and came to south Arkansas to buy about 10,000 acres of virgin timber land for a mere fifteen dollars per acre and later built the sawmill that still operates in Calion. He was an old-fashioned sawmill man, of the "cut out and get out" school that prospered at the turn of the century on the last American frontier of cheap and plentiful virgin hardwood bottomland from Appalachia to the Texas plains. Earlier he had owned and operated mills in Mississippi and Louisiana, but Calion was his last stop. A three-piece-suit frontiersman, he was a gambler and a promoter like so many of his breed; roaring successfully in the 1920s and cut down to size in the 30s, he died disillusioned and near bankruptcy in 1933.

My father was Grandfather's reluctant successor. Neither lumberman by training nor frontiersman by disposition, he abruptly fell heir to a corporate shambles of bank debt and unsold lumber at three southern mills. His good character and innate tenacity kept the company from going under at this most crucial point in its history. He succeeded in holding together the family organization; but above all else he held off the creditors until business revived at the end of the decade. Having saved the company from deadly peril in the Great Depression, his mission accomplished, he promptly returned the company's fortunes largely to the hands of hired managers. The sawmill at Calion, though initially managed by Dad's cousin, Charles Proetz, was after World War II always operated under the management of outsiders. Absentee management with all its drawbacks has been the rule. In 1951 I arrived fresh from college and lumber school.

I alone of all my family think of myself as an Arkansan. My love affair with Arkansas began at age nine on a hot June morning in 1937 aboard the Missouri Pacific Sunshine Special. I raised the curtain in my Pullman berth to see for the first time that relentless stretch of piney woods between Gurdon and El Dorado. The staccato of passing pines was occasionally relieved by small clearings containing a single, unpainted, rough board house, a long porch across its front facing the tracks, an ample dirt yard full of pigs, chickens, and cords of firewood, several black women usually sitting on the porch or washing clothes in the yard, and lots of little black children standing out front by the gate waving at the train.

It was my first glimpse of rural black poverty. Being a city boy, I had heretofore seen only the grimy squalor of row houses and apartments in St. Louis' ghetto, and that only in passing by with rolled up windows. Here there was something different; for poverty then in the rural South tended to be somehow neat and orderly, primitive, with outdoor cistern and privy, coal oil lamps and wood stoves. Most unlike the city, rural poverty seemed private and independent, its single houses set apart from each other, often with large yards and garden plots for its multi-generational families. To my urban eyes these industrious blacks came to epitomize the good earth, the foundation of the rural South, sustained by hard labor and self discipline. Much later, when in my twenties I took over the mill's management, it would be these same proud, strong men, whose houses could be found down every muddy lane and pig trail, who provided a seemingly endless stream of eager mill laborers. They were rugged men with little or no formal schooling, knowledgeable only in the literature of the Bible and the mechanics of one-mule farming, content to accept hard work at minimum wages.

Cheap labor, cheap energy, and cheap timber resources made possible low-priced competitively marketed furniture, flooring, and related hardwood products that helped me to supply the post-war building boom. In terms of labor and raw materials all the mills were on a more or less equal footing. They varied little in how much they paid their laborers (unions were by and large only marginally a factor before the sixties), but differed significantly in how they treated them: at the company store, in credit arrangements on personal and merchandise loans, and as landlords for housing that was usually provided for most employees.

If there was a scandal in the old sawmill towns, it was their abject failure to provide or maintain decent housing for black employees. Viewed by the mill management as a necessary evil to keep labor close at hand, bare frame houses were constructed without amenities and with minimal plumbing, if any. Once constructed, they were allowed to deteriorate with only occasional maintenance. Inadequate foundations settled, porches rotted away, and doors sagged while company landlords looked the other way. In this area, Calion was guilty on all counts; and it wasn't until the mid-Fifties that we acknowledged the deplorable mess over which we presided as landlords and began to repair and sell off all rent houses to their occupants on special terms. It was at this time that we initiated the building of modern prefab houses for employees, contributed to the town's first blacktopping of heretofore dusty gravel streets in Jelly Roll, and supported a plan to bring a federally subsidized waterworks to replace the many shallow water wells in danger of pollution. Recanting its neglectful ways of several decades, the company "got religion" in one fell swoop! It was good politics in a time of general prosperity, commingled with personal guilt.

From the 1950s to the time of this writing a close parallel has existed between the company's activities and my own life; for a closely held family business such as ours is inevitably tied to the personalities and fortunes of those who control it. Having graduated from Washington University in St. Louis with an A.B. in Archeaology in 1950, I was immediately moved to Calion, caught up in the urgencies surrounding a family business in crisis. My father was recovering poorly from a major illness, my only brother just starting college, and the mill, riddled with problems attributed to our absentee ownership was losing money.

It was the onset of eight tumultuous years for me: years of struggle to rebuild the mill from the ground up, to modernize, to acquire more timberland to protect our sources of raw material, and to initiate the more progressive employee-related programs previously mentioned. All of these reforms spelled money and radical changes in company policy, bringing me time and time again into irreconcilable confrontation with my father and his trusted legal counselor, both of whom were alarmed by my programs for tying up capital, assuming bank debt, and accepting short profits until the mill could be revitalized. My will prevailed, but only at the price of my health and the total destruction of my former close relationship with my father. Our endless struggles culminated in 1958 after my brother had acquired several years of experience with the company. My father then agreed to my leaving the company to return to St. Louis to take a master's degree in archaeology, while my brother managed the mill, once more in absentia, from St. Louis.

My father died in 1962, but I remained at Washington University to teach for fifteen years. Shortly after receiving my M.A. in 1960, I became a junior research associate of the distinguished anthropologist, John W. Bennett, with whom I subsequently gained a great deal of field experience in Saskatchewan, Canada. The Canadian research project produced several books for him and for me an incomplete doctoral dissertation that always seemed to get shelved by pressing sawmill business, or at least such is my excuse. Bennett's long-term research project provided me with two intensive summers (1963-64) of field training in the small wheat farming community of Robsart. Here in Saskatchewan (Bennett 1969) our research team developed the interviewing techniques I would later employ in Calion. During my fifteen-year teaching career at

Washington University, I never missed spending all or part of my summer recess in Arkansas working at the mill, always keeping my business interest in tandem with the academic, sometimes like straddling two horses that wanted to run in opposite directions!

Throughout my lifetime I have always cultivated good personal relations with blacks. It has been an attitude flavored with guilt of the certain knowledge that in times of past it was on their backs that my family and I enjoyed the good life. In the turbulent Sixties when the University was under considerable pressure to meet federal guidelines for minority enrollment, as Assistant Dean of the College of Arts and Sciences, I initiated a work-study entry level program for black students that proved very successful in recruiting and retaining economically and academically disadvantaged minorities. Those challenging years took me frequently into St. Louis' largely segregated black high schools, housing projects, and the ghetto community in general, where I was reminded only too frequently of work left undone at Calion. Consequently, in 1974 in a time of academic troubles while federal funding for education and research was in decline, I closed out my academic career and returned to Arkansas to conclude my active years at the mill where I had begun work some twenty-four years before.

The return to Calion provided an opportunity not only to improve conditions at the mill and make amends for past inadequacies, but at the same time to initiate this study, thereby fulfilling my intellectual needs in the anthropological mode. Finally, research in the black community could satisfy a lifelong curiosity and concern about those workers and their families whom I had known, if only superficially, over three generations. Race and position had always constrained our exchanges, but by assuming the role of author and social scientist I found an excuse to enter their homes and their lives more on their own terms. The consequent experiences and friendships that evolved have been personally very rewarding and, I hope, for them as well.

My primary job as proprietor of the mill cannot be forgotten. I concede that the degree and intensity of that involvement precludes complete detachment in this study. Yet, as a trained professional inquirer capable of perceiving and reporting on these facets of the community that reflect negatively upon my own administration or contradict my own views, I can plead a case for concerned detachment. Moreover, my long-term involvement in the community affords insights derived from familiarity and personal acceptance seldom achieved by outside investigators who commonly reside only briefly within the study area.

The field study approach that I have pursued in this book

incorporates the traditional ethnological techniques of long, unstructured interviews and participant observation over a three-year period. Many weeks were spent just sitting and visiting with members of the community, watching, sometimes joining in the routine activities of a household. Interviews, per se, were almost always on a one-to-one basis at times when leisure and privacy afforded uninterrupted and less inhibited exchanges. Tape recorders, questionnaires, and even extensive note-taking were shunned in the belief that these devices distracted or influenced responses. It was my habit during interviews to take notes only in a small notebook, picking up key phrases to facilitate later recall. Revealing quotes were taken down verbatim. I practiced writing rapidly without looking at the page while maintaining eye contact with the informant, thereby avoiding distractions or that "on the record" feeling between the interviewer and informant. This technique, which I had perfected in Saskatchewan, worked well for me so long as I wrote it up while it was still "hot" and small nuances and details were not forgotten.

Since I was no stranger to the community, gaining access was never a problem; and if dealing with "the boss off duty," so to speak, created some distortions and constraints in the question and answer process, I am convinced that this was more than outweighed by long mutual acquaintance and trust. Rarely did I question informants directly about their jobs or other company-related matters. Such information came inferentially. Of course, as in any field study situation, there was an element of mutual exploitation: I in pursuit of a good book, striving for revealing, quotable material; and in return, although I never paid for an interview directly, I was from time to time tapped for small loans that practically never seemed to get repaid. Ultimately, any acid test of candor and rapport came from the informant's willingness to reveal personally sensitive, sometimes incriminating evidence concerning drug taking or dealing, welfare cheating, and other covert activities wherein their anonymity had to be assured. With a few notable exceptions when informants took advantage of a once-in-a-lifetime chance to tell me off or "bad mouth" the company on their own front porch (I tried to thank them for their candor), there was commonly a tacit if unspoken understanding that talking about sensitive company business could nullify that parity of our relationship, and thereby compromise an otherwise easy exchange of information and ideas. With this single inhibition, interviews ranged widely over the field of human concern. Lastly, I tried to structure interviews to the degree that I could obtain parallel accounts of the same event, cross-checking data for accuracy and differences in points of view.

This verification technique had been stressed by Bennett in Saskatchewan and served me well again here in Calion.

I have attempted to look at community and families from both a contemporary and historical perspective, frequently profiling members of three generations in the same family. At Calion the continuity in mill ownership, a history of labor peace and mutual cooperation, an expanding enterprise in a small town with low unemployment except for the decade of the Great Depression, all conspired to make the community atypical, and its history uniquely important, setting it apart from the chronic American problem of urban poverty and unemployment. In a sense, this gives a "best case" quality to our little community. What if the rest of America had not suffered the traumatic sharp slides into recurrent unemployment, especially for its black minority? What if the rest of the country had been as successfully insulated, geographically and socially, from the depressed ghettos' drug culture and violent crime? And what if the rest of the country's blacks had, as a result of legislative fiat, been as rapidly integrated into the economic mainstream? Calion's problems are benign by comparison with the urban ghettos I have read about or visited. Calion, then, may provide us with just such a "best case" example of black working-class community striving upwards toward economic equality and out of the backwoods into contemporary mass society. Therein lies its special merit.

A last note on the organization of the book itself, in which I have consciously worked toward three principal goals: first, to provide an overview of a rapidly changing black community; and second, to elucidate these swiftly changing attitudes and life styles by means of individual profiles organized into the divisions of three living generations. This narrative profile technique was chosen to feature the explicit, sometimes condensed statements of the informants, thereby affording the reader the opportunity to experience and appreciate the articulate, often dramatic verbal skills prevalent in this black community. Lastly, I hope to provide the reader with a straightforward, unexpurgated view of the black community as I recorded and perceived it at a distance from the political pressures and conventional wisdom of academic professionalism. Within the limits of my own background and capabilities, I have tried to present this black community as much as possible as it sees itself, rejoicing in its virtues but unafraid to reveal its vices.

Unfortunately there are no satisfactory, locally generated statistics available for the community. Social Services data are virtually useless for our purposes since they are kept only for the sprawling county as a whole, including the city of El Dorado. U.S. Census data for such small commmunities as Calion is adulterated by statistical averaging. Nonetheless, I have tried to firm up conclusive statements by using percentile surveys, for in a community of only eighty-plus households it was possible to conduct one hundred percent canvasses for certain key data. This is, after all, a saturation study of a small neighborhood population.

The profiles technique which I have employed was inspired by the work of the late Oscar Lewis (1959). And, although as an anthropologist, I could not escape the influence of Robert Redfield's studies of little communities as a cultural unit (1955), I concur with Lewis in avoiding Redfield's arbitrary topical divisions of culture and society. In Jelly Roll "community" speaks through the opinions and actions of its denizens, and their culture is their shared understanding and traditions.

By dividing the individuals interviewed into three generational groups, I have attempted to dramatize the degree and rapidity of culture change in this community. I have labeled this change "deculturation," a chronic form of an ongoing, worldwide loss of ethnic traditions and identity. Certainly the old folks in Jelly Roll never use the word deculturation, but they nonetheless categorize in their own words loss of traditional styles, customs, and skills, values that have been discarded without substitute, except in the sense that the amorphous culture of mass society and the mass media's ever-changing eclecticism is an alternative culture.

I have concentrated on the cultural content of a neighborhood community while consciously avoiding more than a superficial concern with social organization and social history. In so doing, I have chosen to ignore not only a major feature of anthropological craft, but also an aspect of Jelly Roll with which I have had close contact for the past thirty-five years. Potentially, their social structure and social history is a fascinating whole other book; but, in concurrence with the theoretical perspectives of Lewis (1961), I have subordinated social structure in this volume to overriding cultural and economic factors.

Although the working-class black family continues to be threatened from the outside, we can no longer ignore the compelling evidence that there is trouble within. One fact is certain nationally, that female-headed households continue to grow both in absolute numbers and as a percentage of the whole black population (Matusow 1984). The black matrifocal family continues to proliferate on early pregnancies, which when carried to delivery as thier culture encourages, potentiates a whole new generation of dependent, culturally deprived and economically ill-equipped poor.

Hopefully, in a modest way *Jelly Roll* will contribute to our understanding of this dilemma.

CHAPTER 2

Mill Town

A Small Industrial Community

Interlacing the vast pine forest of the Deep South are many great rivers and meandering streams that carry off the heavy, subtropical rains that have shaped the topography below the Mason-Dixon Line. Unlike the wide, silt-laden rivers to the east that have produced the deep, rich soils that characterize the Mississippi Delta, southwest Arkansas's light sandy lands, once the submerged bottoms of inland seas, are drained by narrow, often turbulent rivers that have produced bottomlands ill-suited to large-scale clearing and leveling or construction of protective levees. Consequently, when the Deep South developed a prosperous and cultured plantation society based upon cotton, and later rice and soybeans as well, Arkansas, on its western fringe, did not uniformly benefit from the rich deep soils that supported this society. Thus much of the state's economy supported only the plantations' backwoods cousins, largely consisting of subsistence farmers and sawmillers. In lieu of the lordly slave estates was a more flexible, open, and westward-looking pioneer economy. The spirit and skills of latter-day frontiersmen still prevail in the pine lands of Arkansas and are evident in this country's preoccupation with fishing, hunting, camping, and woods lore. The rugged naturalist spirit, the love of the out-of-doors, and the pursuit of game have become an enduring tradition of a male society of woodsmen, both black and white.

Moreover, running through the preceding generations of small farmers is the tradition of black and white working harmoniously, if not equally, side by side and living fence to fence. The small towns of Arkansas, as a whole, cared not a whit about zoning laws or social isolation and grew up with a vibrant scramble of commercial and residential property without segregation by propinquity of caste or class. Arkansas, in the Southern tradition, practiced strict segregation in certain public places, but little in private. Through economic necessity and social precedent, black and white shared hard work and low wages, pursuing each in his own way the more bountiful life not by means of his purse, but rather through the unspoiled, game-rich natural world that was just beyond his doorstep.

The easy dialogue and cooperation between the races should not be confused with any kind of premature equality, for as a former Arkansas Senator once noted, "In the South they don't care how close a Negro gets as long as he doesn't get too high, while in the North they don't care how high he gets as long as he doesn't get too close." In Arkansas this has been demonstrated by the historic white dominance of skilled jobs, apprentice-based occupations, and almost all categories of higher-paying jobs in general. When oil was discovered in South Arkansas in the Twenties, the dirty, hazardous but very lucrative jobs in the oil fields and refineries went almost exclusively to whites. Economic discrimination was always very much a part of the Arkansas scene, but the historic precedents for close working relationships between the races clearly facilitated real compliance with the civil rights legislation in the 1960s and 70s.

By industrialized yardsticks of progress Arkansas has been perennially ranked at or near the bottom of the states. Be it per capita income, plumbing and housing standards, average number of years in school, production of goods and services, hospital beds, or number of doctors per hundred thousand persons, all statistics point to Arkansas as a backward state (1980 Census, Supplementary Report). In fact, being from Arkansas "up North or back East" required a thick skin and a good set of defenses to parry the derisive quips and mush-mouthed pejoratives that predictably came our way. It has only been recently that the Sun Belt image has largely replaced that of slavers, bootleggers, and redneck farmers. The state's geographic separation from the metroplexes to the North and East, the infertility of its western soil, and the ruggedness of much of its terrain have afforded it a long latency period. The extensive pine forests stretching from one end of the state to the other are still the economically best use of the land, insuring its protection from bulldozer and plow, sustaining along its intricate webbing of rivers, swamps, lakes, and streams, waters at least relatively free from factory and urban wastes, while assuring mercifully low population densities.

Backwardness has become a sought-after attribute where retirees in particular, beset with the maladies of progress, come to seek a more tranquil conclusion to their lives. Thus through an irony of fate, Arkansas has become a sanctuary for many of its long-time detractors.

Calion, population 638, on the banks of the Ouachita River, is one of these bucolic settings, surrounded still by hundreds of thousands of acres of timberland. Like the river itself, the town of Calion is something of a meandering unplanned community divided in the middle by the Rock Island railroad tracks, the highway on the west, and swampy Calion Lake to the south. Its angled streets with closely spaced rows of houses have the disconcerting habit of suddenly dead-ending in patches of overgrown forest from which may emerge at any time, day or night, gun-toting hunters with their dogs at heel. Much of the year the streets are alive with gun-racked pickup trucks and four-wheel-drive vehicles for negotiating the muddy river bottom roads. On any fair day a most common sight along the streets and paths of the town is black women and elderly men with pails and fishing poles heading off to any number of favorite fishing holes on the lakes or river that nearly encircle the town.

The sawmill, lumber yard, furniture plant, and office extend roughly westward from the river bank. Past the office and gate to the plant premises, the town begins with two streets at right angles to each other, Mill and Thomas Streets. There, except for a smattering of white residences near the office, is the primary black settlement of the town.

"Jelly Roll" is the black oldsters' nickname for this original black neighborhood that grew up on the street next to the sawmill. As a practical matter throughout this book I shall refer to "Calion" when speaking of the town as a whole, and "Jelly Roll" when dealing with the black community within the town. The neighborhood encompassing the study is basically small and compact with the houses laid out on narrow but deep lots fifty to sevety-five feet across the front, lending an air of crowded intimacy. The houses are mostly frame with ample front porches and small front yards often surrounded by shrubs and flowering vines, but the condition of individual residences shows great variation from brightly and perfectly manicured to terminally run down.

To the south of the Jelly Roll quarters is Main Street with its predictable commercial cluster of stores, no more than two groceries, a filling station, a post office and city hall, Masonic Lodge, a boarded up little cafe, and a closet-sized barbershop, all white owned and operated businesses. Also, in typical small town design, the extension of Main Street between U.S. Highway #167 and the abandoned Rock Island tracks is lined with the best homes, new and old, brick and frame, adjacent to the town's three white churches. Beyond the city limits, where the sale of alcoholic beverages is permitted, are two beer joints, a small one on the highway and one with a large bi-racial clientele on Calion Lake at Crab Apple Point, within blocks of the city limits.

The paucity of commercial activity in Calion reflects the proximity (12 miles) to the city of El Dorado with a population of 25,000. In the town of Calion itself, the convenience and credit-extending grocery and general merchandise store, as well as the more distant beer emporiums, get a good play locally; but, except at mail time and when the mill whistle lets out a shift of workers, the main part of town with its absense of sidewalks, a square, or place to sit, quickly transacts its limited business to return to sleepy indifference. In total contrast, the streets of Jelly Roll are almost always alive with activity: children playing at the roadside, loitering adults and casual strollers, especially around the centrally located Willow Grove Baptist Church. A few doors down is Clara's Sandwich Shop, where children buy candy and a Coke or mill workers pick up barbeque. Up and down both Thomas and Mill Streets in Jelly Roll is a steady coming and going at certain houses that sell beer, cigarettes, and candy, all unfettered by "the Law," taxes or red tape. Hence, Jelly Roll, day or night, is a lively place to be where street life is the thing.

The lumber company is the town's only industry, employing approximately 125 persons, of whom over half are residents of Calion with the remainder coming from nearby towns and countryside. Paralleling Calion's racial mix, which was 47% black in the 1980 census, the company's work force is 59% black (74/125 on January 1, 1983).

The company operates a sawmill, lumber yard, and furniture parts plant, and, because of lighter work available in the latter, the total work force includes twenty-nine women, half (15/29) of whom are black. In a number of cases both husband and wife, father and son, brother and sister, etc. are working for the company, thereby creating both a family atmosphere and a degree of clannishness at work. Even though this small town consanguinity sometimes produces conflict and conspiratorial complications, it is also a cementing and harmonizing force on the job and in the town and may be a significant factor overall in explaining the town's relatively low level of serious crime. However, full employment is probably the overriding factor.

The company's family-owned and operated base has provided a traditional paternalism that has also been a positive factor in the community's stability as previously discussed, and has provided adequate housing for many employees since the 1950s. The company continues to sell lots and prefab houses with long-term financing through the payroll deduction plan. Through company auspices, employees may also secure legal counseling, interest-free loans, as well as the usual corporate package of life, health, and retirement benefits on a par with the large national corporations. Labor relations have been, on the whole, harmonious. The furniture plant was unionized by the A.F.L., Affiliated Furniture Workers of America, in 1969. There has been only one brief strike of less than two weeks duration in 1970. With continued union pressure and the competition for labor among the surrounding mills, the company's wage and incentive pay package is higher than that of most of its competitors.

Both town and job bring blacks and whites physically into contact day in and day out. In like manner, all the town's children mount the same big yellow school buses five days a week to be transported to Norphlet, another nearby small town which acts as the region's consolidated school district and where educational facilities are completely integrated for students and staff alike. In Calion it is common to see blacks and whites standing together talking on street corners or conducting personal business, or sitting side by side on the river bank, at the mill exchanging casual conversation, even playing cards or dominoes together during breaks at the furniture plant or on the lumber yard. From time to time there will be a much-talked-about incident of interracial dating or cohabitation; but beyond these occasional personal intersections still lurk the rigidities of the segregated past. New economic opportunities for blacks have produced what are essentially two parallel societies — side by side, almost touching but not really together. In areas of choice, blacks and whites continue for the most part to shun each other's company except in long-established ways. Territoriality, without the odious signs marked "Colored" or "White Only," remains as part of an informal and unspoken code on conduct, especially in mixed gathering places where blacks and whites are inclined to congregate separately, such as the beach on Calion Lake, certain picnic tables, and shade trees at the beer emporium at Crab Apple Point, and the benches around the fire station and city hall.

Old attitudes of subservience and deference on the part of blacks have been replaced by new attitudes of indifference or hostility toward whites, especially those whites that live with them in the same town. This is most often expressed by blank stares at whites, a gesture apparent even among the smallest children who play along the streets of Jelly Roll and routinely wave and call out to almost every passing car with black occupants, but stare with pretended sightlessness at whites whom they obviously know. An element of this sort of hostility exists even in the street's black market mini-economy, which openly bypasses the white man's stores and taxes.

A major factor underlying this pervasive and continuing racial antagonism is a general feeling, openly expressed by many blacks, that despite economic strides locally and nationally, "it's still a white man's world" wherein whites remain adamantly entrenched in the seats of power, except in the Union Local currently controlled by blacks. These facts of life have not been lost upon them. Economic reform is still in progress, and economic reform is not all, as a variety of more subtle inequities continue to curdle relations between the races.

Whites have countered black hostility with their own brand of negativism largely directed at black welfare recipients whom they characterize as a privileged class anointed in their own backyard by liberal Northern politicians. Their target is a conspicuously idle segment of the local black population (whites tend to keep welfare benefits quietly out of sight), "well heeled and well wheeled" that cruise the town's streets while the whites "slave away to keep the niggers in fun and food stamps." Moreover, these same blacks often receive the blame for tax bracket creep, Social Security increases, inflation, foreign competition, and all the other ills that affect the country in general and their paychecks in particular. In subsequent profiles, we shall look at both sides of this welfare picture.

The town of Calion has a somewhat seedy look, an impression that discounts many attractive homes and gardens interspersed among black and white neighborhoods alike. The overall impression clearly signals to even the casual viewer that Calion is not uniformly concerned with the suburban game of keeping up with the Joneses. It is important to note that housing here is a deceptive indication of income level; for, in this rural setting, outdoor living, hunting and fishing, and their related paraphernalia often take precedence over better homes and gardens. This is even more characteristic of the black than the white community, where many families that not too long ago had to "live poor" in terms of physical facilities continue, in their present prosperity, to do so by choice. While time to accrue equity is sometimes a factor, differences in priorities and black family organization are far more important. Often, as we shall see, in the black community kinsmen may make heavy claims upon the income of certain housholds. Even families with two or more wage earners and combined incomes in excess of $20,000 per year may be "livin' poor," caught in the web of kinship obligations: i.e., raising children by previous consorts, the care of their children's children, while parents, uncles, aunts, brothers, sisters and even cousins, or adopted kin, feel free to call upon their widely known resources or good credit (Stack 1974).

In the past decade, blacks have risen rapidly towards achieving job parity, holding on January 1, 1983 45% of the skilled jobs at the mill at an annual gross pay ranging from $15,000 to $23,000. The Jelly Roll community supplies the company with some fifty-four employees, which is 41% of the company's work force. Of all the households in Jelly Roll (84), forty-six (55%) have one or more company employees. Of these eleven (24%) have incomes in the $18,000-$32,000 range, twenty-one (46%) in excess of $15,000 as compared to the State of Arkansas's median income of $12,214 per household in 1979; and all full-time employees exceed $10,500 on an unskilled wage of six dollars per hour or more. In Arkansas in 1979, by comparison, 55% of all black families had incomes of less than $10,000.

In summary, we are dealing with a high employment black working-class neighborhood with a nucleus of more affluent skilled and two-income families. It is important to emphasize the exclusively blue collar nature of this community which, through the years, has steadily moved a growing number of its offspring up and out to achieve "better jobs in the big city." This includes a steady migration of the more ambitious, adventuresome, and better educated to such far away cities as Los Angeles and Chicago. The U.S. Armed Services has proved to be a vital springboard for young men, and now women in growing numbers, who felt constrained or unrewarded "sawmilling in the backwoods."

The homes of many residents proudly display the service photographs and regalia of one or more departed sons or daughters. Local migrations are frequent among those who attain high school diplomas, or better yet, college, or technical school training. This group moves regularly to El Dorado, Little Rock or beyond as teachers, nurses, computer operators, etc. They also return frequently to continue to play and enjoy a high-profile role in the community. On any Sunday or holiday, and especially at funerals, these returnees are featured as honored guests with much neighborhood fanfare and excitement.

Conspicuous in the residential pattern of Jelly Roll are the large number of retirees' homes (21/84). Their predominantly run-down appearance reflects the limited incomes and less prosperous times for blacks here in the past; and their relatively large numbers confirm the long term outward migration pattern of the young. Subsidized public housing in El Dorado has also attracted a number of younger families from job holders in Calion who might otherwise have settled in Jelly Roll.

Exceeding the national trend among blacks in sharply reduced family size (Scanzoni 1971), Jelly Roll now averges only 3.2 persons per household (267 persons in 84 units). This is still higher than the 1980 state average per household of 2.74 persons, but a radical departure from the "old sawmill days." Only eight households had more than six occupants (7-10) and except for one, these were all extended families. The childbearing issue in Jelly Roll has long since switched from too many babies to support, to the more complex questions surrounding when and to whom babies are being born.

In addition to the volatile demands of kinship, there are demands of life style. The old folks in Jelly Roll like to divide families into one of two categories: those that are "livin' high," and those that are "livin' with the spirit." The former life style, while widely admired and emulated, especially by the younger generation, with heavy emphasis on clothes, cars, and stereos, inevitably takes a heavy toll on the pocketbook, as its pleasures are quickly consumed or discarded. However, it is not uncommon in a lifetime to embrace these two life styles consecutively, experiencing religion and conservatism along with the aging process.

From the point of view of the churches, both black and white, the town provides a natural battleground for the sacred and profane, and on Sundays the preachers regularly announce the casualties and the saved. On one block of Main Street are three large white churches; while in Jelly Roll, strategically located near the center of the battleground, is the red brick Willow Grove Baptist Church representing the town's largest black congregation (there are also two other very small churches with a more evangelical bent). Willow Grove Baptist has an official census of over ninety parishioners, an impressively large segment of the town's total black population; but as a practical matter the number, except for "the Easter egg hide and bonnet stroll" is no more than half active members. Nonetheless, the church, with its elderly residents as respected deacons, its Mission Sisters who actively bring aid and cheer to the sick, distressed, and shut-ins throughout the Jelly Roll community, and the well-attended children's Sunday School, provides all together an active symbol as well as a repository for traditional black culture. And if the "livin' high" crowd dominates the streets six days a week, on Sunday it becomes a study in black suits, white cotton, and polyester, reminiscent of the community's past dominance by pastors and deacons. As we shall subsequently observe, the turn of events in the recent history of emancipation, and economic equality in particular, has shocked as much as satisfied Jelly Roll's elders, spawning, as they perceive it, Satan's beachhead in the promised land.

The older generation from whom we shall hear first was in its youth in the 1930s, in the prime of life in the 1940s and 1950s and went into retirement in the 1960s and 1970s. Their warm memories of the past, especially the Thirties, the decade of drought and the Great Depression, is no doubt colored by nostalgia for their lost youth. It is generally agreed, however, that this golden age of self reliance, cooperation, and good fellowship came to an end some time in the late 1950s. This brings us to the question of what significant changes occurred between 1930 and 1960 that so profoundly affected the character of the community.

In a very real sense, the little town of Calion was not pulled into the mainstream of the national political economy until the late 1950s. Wages were still low, and job segregation militantly shut out blacks from the higher-paying skilled or even semi-skilled positions, and the engulfing civil rights movement of the 1960s was before then only an occasional Sunday murmur from the more radical black evengelist preachers. In short, while the mill expanded and prospered in the post-war years, black labor, drawn in abundant supply from small surrounding farms, made only modest gains in real wages and was not swept into the mainstream of national prosperity until the decade of the 1960s. The local black population tended to live as they had lived since the Civil War in large multi-generational families (Billingsley 1968), often underemployed, sending most of their youth to the big cities of the North. In Calion, as elsewhere in the South, they continued to practice a mixed economy that supplemented low cash wages with garden-plot farming and the raising of livestock, especially chickens and pigs.

For one who has had a part in this community since the late 1940s, I can unequivocally confirm the remembrances of the old timers as to appearance of the town. Vacant lots and tens of acres of land adjacent to the Jelly Roll community that have long since reverted to tall weeds and forest was, as late as the 1950s, a continuous chain of individual garden plots, each worked by local residents and involving the attentive labor of the entire family. The old timers look back fondly on the "open look" where one could easily see better than a mile from the Rock Island Railroad tracks to Highway #167. This garden community provided the standard of rural beauty for several generations. Only the youth of today have "always lived in this bramble patch" and remember it not at all.

Today only three or four large gardens are being worked in Jelly Roll, for the 1960s brought civil rights legislation and a building boom that raised wages much higher in the black community. It became no longer necessary to supplement incomes with home-grown produce. Rather, it became prestigious to set aside the plow and the hoe and sit back or go fishing after the four o'clock whistle blew; only those who gardened for pleasure, mostly widows and retirees, kept up the old skills. With the foreclosure of the mixed economy came an end to the interpersonal exchanges of goods and services that were the bond of the communal spirit. When neighbors no longer traded butchered hogs for sorghum molasses or canned turnips, the foundation of their relationships atrophied, becoming mere form without function.

Ironically, the black community's successful struggle toward economic equality and their merger into a cash economy saw a simultaneous ebbing of the common experiences of their folk culture. Previously united by the trauma of the Great Depression, sharing a barter economy in adversity and experiencing the common denials of racial discrimination, they also spiritually and emotionally reached the high point of their lives. For they were whole then, a people and their God successfully prevailing in the face of many adversities, one color, one faith with common experiences and common goals.

We may conclude that it is with wisdom and clear insight that the old timers, with whom we have conversed, look back upon their past. For they have confronted and judged the inadequacies of material prosperity when purchased, and the price is always high, with the diminution of even the most transient spiritual and social things. Spiritual identification with the group and social commitment to be one's neighbor's keeper are highly gratifying states. The meaningful congregation of one's cherished group may well be one of man's most ancient and rewarding experiences. The old timers knew it well. Granted, they idealize the past, but they also know from comparative experience exactly what they have lost. Their offspring, on the other hand, are caught between half-remembered youth and the contemporary fragmented society they have known as adults. Only too often they are thus trapped between the imperfect memory of the former and an uncomfortable adaption to the latter. They are our generation in transition that we shall hear from subsequently.

This book begins with the old timers and then proceeds to examine the group in middle age, and concludes with youth, rather arbitrarily designated as those thirty and younger. Nineteen profiles of families or individuals are included. Over seventy persons were interviewed for a minimum of several hours, sometimes over many days or weeks, even months in several cases, during an intense three years of inquiry in the community. Every effort has been made to provide the reader with a balanced cross section of residents. It should be noted that except for one pastor and one paralegal this is strictly a working-class community, a mill town only twelve miles from the service center of El Dorado (population 25,000). With the two noted exceptions, those who have gone beyond a high school education to become professionals, businessmen, teachers, etc., have routinely emigrated to El Dorado or beyond.

The nineteen profiles of individuals or families are more or less equally divided 6-7-6 among the divisions of age. Admittedly, the length and detail of individual profiles vary greatly based upon interest and the rapport established with different informants.

Family structure in Jelly Roll is not easily categorized. Standard residential typologies by homes of retirees, married couples, divorcees, and singles do not fit neatly here, where the shifting sands of cohabitation and the interlocking alliances of extended families defy conventional organizational schemes. Therefore, I have elected to provide the reader with a complete household survey of all eighty-four Jelly Roll residences (see Appendix A). This survey may be summarized as follows:

- 19 Residences of Retirees (aged 62 and older)
- 16 Extended Family Residences (three or four generations usually but sometimes only grandparents and grandchildren)
- 25 Married or Cohabitating (2 years or more) Couples (below age 62, with or without children)
- 20 Men Living Alone or With Temporary Consorts (less than 2 years)
- 4 Women Living Alone or With Temporary Consorts (less than 2 years)

This organization scheme is obviously prejudiced toward a stable model of our community. By including cohabitants of two years or more with married couples and viewing the extended family, though often stressed by returning children, as basically a strong institution of social support, we infer that only the last two categories, men and women alone or with temporary consorts, tend to be "unstable." Yet as residential units, these last two categories represent 30% (24/84) of the total, a significantly large proportion. Moreover, the question of the relative stability of extended families and cohabitating couples will be a central concern of this book.

Consequently, I have featured multi-generational households in six profiles from a total of sixteen in the community (37.5%). These residences, often the home of an older parent or parents, constitute the largest population aggregate in the community (100). They are of particular interest since they provide safe havens for returning daughters, often with babies and young children in tow, who will "leave the kids with grandma for a while" and return alone to a job and a man in town or city. Sometimes young and not so young sons and daughters return alone as dropouts from an ended affair or marriage in order to reorder their lives before launching out again. The extended family household also plays an important ongoing role in the lives of local sons and daughters who have single apartments or "live-in" arrangements nearby.

Where divorce in white society usually portends at least temporary isolation of the separated partners and the loneliness of single-parent custody for their children, the black extended family frequently offers an alternative of nurture and sanctuary as well as garrulous reinforcement by a host of kinfolks wherein feelings of abandonment are minimized (Bass et al, 1982).

Married couples and longer-term cohabitants constitute the largest residential segment (25 units) of our community and are represented by seven profiles for a 28% coverage. However, only minimally represented by two profiles (10%) are the unexpectedly large number of men (20) ostensibly living alone or only briefly with partners. Does this group reflect, here in rural Arkansas, just another segment of the national trend at all levels of society towards living single with casual affairs? Or is this, instead, further evidence in Jelly Roll of the male macho cult that prizes brief, competitive conquests and shuns long-term commitments? This latter interpretation is suggested throughout this book, especially in the profile of con man, George Wesley. Then, too, this category of single males may be, at least in part, a random collection of bachelors, those only temporarily divorced or separated, in addition to several widowers. If such is the case, only their reluctance or slowness, vis a vis the women, to take another mate is an issue of interest.

The welfare question will be extensively aired as a major preoccupation of the neighborhood. For a full employment community such as Calion, the use of welfare seems quite pervasive (at least 18 of 84 households), especially among extended families. Five of our nineteen profiles or 26.3% are on welfare as compared to 21.4% identified in the community as a whole.

Although all names have been routinely changed in every profile, I have taken added precautions and used diversionary disguises including altered descriptions of residences, occupation, family size and certain personal characteristics in order to preserve the anonymity of those informants who could be made vulnerable or embarressed by exposure. Thus the confidentiality of certain interviews has been protected at the expense of the accuracy of certain empirical detail. This is especially true of chapters in which welfare irregularities or the sale of controlled substances could create serious problems for the informants. Where fictitious embellishment was necessary for disguise, I have attempted always to employ parallel situations from my knowledge of other black communities in order to retain realistic perspectives. In instances where drug dealing and other serious crimes are involved, total anonymity was maintained by not individually describing participants, as in the Chapters "Rappin' with the Boys on the Street" and "Talk about Town."

PART I

The Old Timers

Folk Ways and Traditional Culture Under Siege

CHAPTER 3

Sylvester Malone

Living Memories Back on the Farm

Sylvester and Eartha Malone are in their seventies, but neither has the slightest intention of retiring any time soon to become "porch sitters." Sylvester went to work at the mill in 1950. He was a fireman stoking the sawmill boilers until he retired from the "heavy job" just a few years ago when he became a night watchman, which he describes as light work. "But you can't just loaf around on this job with nine stations to punch on this time clock I carry. You see, I've always got my boss strapped to my shoulder." His wife, Eartha, is also retired as a cook for the company's logging operation; now she also has a "light job" just cooking for one family. This energetic older couple, who between them have made a good living for many years, nonetheless live in one of the plainest, even rundown, houses on Mill Street, demonstrating that in a black community like Jelly Roll, residence is, more often than not, a low priority concern. Sylvester always drives a late-model car, takes an annual trip with his wife to see relatives in California, gives generously to the church at his birthplace on Champagnolle Hill, and lavishes money, again in the black tradition, upon his seven children and many grandchildren, two of whom live with him.

Their annual visit to Los Angeles is a bitter-sweet event primarily undertaken to keep up with children and other relatives living there. Sylvester describes it as Br'er Rabbit's trip to the big city:

> This skittish old rabbit don't like to get shook to pieces on a bus for three days, and he don't like to stay scared to death on a plane that might go down at any minute! Now those pretty people runnin' the plane try to tame you with drinks and food so you won't be thinkin' about what a dangerous and foolish thing you're doin'. But I stay in a sweat the whole trip. And I don't like nothin' about L.A. either; too fast and noisy for this old man, too many fire trucks and police cars. I'm like that hard-to-tame rabbit; everytime an acorn falls, he jumps. I can't sleep out there at all. Don't sleep too well in Calion, but I can go out to the church yard on Champagnolle Hill where I was born and sleep under that big oak tree any old afternoon.

Sylvester is a man of superior intellect, a master of language. He speaks rapidly with a song-like cadence to his voice. He is an insightful man, a shrewd judge of human nature who, given another time and another place, might have achieved a lofty position in society. But as fate would have it, he was born black on a remote farm on the upper reaches of the Ouachita River in 1910, father unknown, to an indifferent mother. He recalls being taken over and raised by the white Henderson family who owned and worked the large Champagnolle plantation. On the farm the work was hard, the hours long, discipline was strict and unyielding; but Sylvester dotes upon those idyllic days of his childhood and youth as though he were himself the pampered heir to a great estate. The fact of the matter is that he developed deep emotional ties to the Henderson family with whom he was raised like their own, spending his childhood in their house. This cabin, typical for its time and place in the rural South, had an open-air covered hallway down its center roof line that divided the building into two living units. One half, containing the kitchen, also housed a family of black servants, while the other half contained the bedrooms and living quarters for the white owners. Sylvester lived in the former half of the Henderson home and was thus in constant close association with the Henderson family and their own children.

The farm was exceptionally large for the hill country of Arkansas and was marvelously situated by over-reaching bluffs and valleys on the banks of the meandering Ouachita River. The Hendersons employed eight black families and had fifteen mules and three horses to cultivate the fields and clear new land each winter, for unfertilized sandy soil rapidly lost its fertility. The farm was located immediately adjacent to the oldest settlement in the region, the historic Champagnolle Landing, where on the spring rise the paddle wheel boats journeyed up from the Mississippi River bringing trade goods, sugar, and farm implements in exchange for bales of cotton. With a large dockside warehouse, Bell's gin house, two stores, a church, and a number of large cabins, Champagnolle was a "pretty thick settlement for these backwoods" and a picturesque farming community to be sure.

It was here under the concerned, watchful eye of the Hendersons that Sylvester grew into manhood. He was deeply attached to the family with whom he lived as one of their own. "Mrs. Henderson treated all of us children the same, black and white; and if she felt a difference she was sharp enough to keep it from us so that we never knew or felt it."

Sylvester's memories overflowed with joy of living in this rambling farm house, of work and simple pleasures: the tactile sense of rough-hewn planks under foot, the smell of rich pine wood and hay barns, fragrant tobacco leaves and honey pressed to make long round plugs of chewing tobacco, the eggs collected each day and layed out on the Henderson's bed in preparation for boxing, the smells of the smoke house, and the bountiful food that emerged with such regularity from Mrs. Henderson's kitchen.

The farm was run with an authoritarian but apparently reassuring benevolence:

> Mrs. Henderson was not only a real cook, she was a really sweet woman. She reasoned with you, never scolded, never angry or raised her voice. I remember one day when I was just a tall boy, after noon dinner, she said, 'Son, go down to the tomato patch and hoe them til they're clean.' I just nodded my head for I was angry and sleepy, and I didn't mind at all. I slept till after 3:00 p.m. and never went down to tend those tomatoes a single lick.
>
> But soon I started to regret it. I knew it was comin', though several days had passed and she hadn't said a thing or acted one bit upset. Then one afternoon several days later she caught me alone, set me down and said, 'Son, the other day I asked you to go out and hoe the tomatoes. Now I won't be with you much longer, so hear what I have to say. It wouldn't have taken you more than thirty minutes to hoe those tomatoes with a will; but against your will you can only fail. How many rooms in this house? ["Seven," I answered.] Well, some day I may ask you to raise up the corner of this house. And if I do, I want you to come to the task with a will. Grab ahold of the corner and raise up with all your might. And even if you don't budge it an inch, you can come to me and say I tried with all my heart and all my might. That's all I ask of you.'
>
> Now I often think on what she said. When I was in that sawmill boiler room and it was so hot in the summertime,

sometimes I thought I'd pass out, then her words gave me strength to continue the job . . .

Now Mr. Henderson was partial to me, too. No doubt about it. I shaved him every day until he died. He named my first three children with his family names. He didn't have Mrs. Henderson's good disposition. He could be cruel, say terrible things to you, but I loved him still. No, I don't have to guess about it, I loved them and they loved me; he deeded me twenty acres of his own land, and we lived the good life down there on the river.

Life on the farm had a measured rhythm of seasonal work and play. Every afternoon when the sun was low, Sylvester pumped the long oak troughs full of water for the mules to drink and waited for the men to return from the field. There were eggs to be gathered and regular chores around the house and barns. The farm was nearly self-sufficient with its own blacksmith shop to forge farm tools and wagon wheels, a grist mill, and a carpentry shop where among other things comfortable plaited three-vine chairs were made for all. Smokehouse, fruit cellar, and barn stored the diverse harvest, and during the more leisurely winter season everyone went hunting, did some fishing and collected firewood, while the more enterprising split fence rails at three dollars a hundred.

And so Sylvester spent his youth, comfortable and content with the simple farm life until in 1931, when he was twenty years old, Mrs. Henderson, his devoted foster mother, came down with tuberculosis and was hospitalized in El Dorado, where she remained for fifteen years before she died of the disease (as did her three sisters and three bothers). After she left the farm, Sylvester was charged with the personal care of Mr. Henderson, who was by then getting up in years, and had none of his children left on the farm to look after him. In this new position of prominence and authority in the big house, Sylvester began to entertain thoughts of marriage. And for the first time in his life he became intensely conscious of the prejudices and ambiguities attached to his race and position:

Injustice comes to you when you think about the outside world. Three sawmills boomin' down the road at Calion. More traffic comin' down Champagnolle Road. It made this colored boy think on what was goin' on about him. I had always gotten on extra good with white people and whites had protected us pretty good. They'd say 'don't fool with my niggers.' They'd stand for you if you got in trouble with the law. We were taught to always honor the authority of the whites. That wasn't always easy when any fool could see the differences between what the whites had and the colored didn't have. Was it God's will that color should make such a difference? Doesn't the black cow give the same milk as the white? It was hard for me when me and my sister would be left working in the fields and the white children would be passin' by on the way to school. They looked so pretty! We colored only went to school for two months in the summer while they went the rest of the year, you see. . . . Our people didn't have nothin'. We had to work the crops on half shares, and that was unjust. There was no chance of making more than a bare living. Only the many poor whites around us took the sting out of it some.

There were other injustices and troubles. Sometimes the colored people suffered from the greed of merchants and other powerful whites. And I won't soon forget how the colored suffered sorely from the clap [gonorrhea]. There wasn't any penicillin in those days and the clap got somethin' fierce. I never had it myself, nothin' but the flu now and again, but I've seen some miserable folks afflicted. Some stank with it if you passed them on the street.

Now old Dr. Baff used to specialize in treating it. He made up his own medicine, mostly blue ointment, I guess. It wouldn't cure you, but it must have given those boys some relief the way they flocked to see him. Now old Dr. Baff lived alone on the river. He had a fine cabin settin' up on big cypress logs tied off to trees at the corners. They just floated that cabin high and dry whenever the river flooded out of the bank. He just set there on the river fishin' and waitin' for these miserable old boys, colored and plenty whites too, that would come a-clomping up the river to get their treatments.

It seemed strange that a clap doctor would live in one of the prettiest places you'd ever see. You could walk there up the river from the mill in less than ten minutes, across Chapelle Slough on a huge cypress foot log. Now that deep, dark slough was surrounded by some of the tallest cypress trees I've ever seen. Then the path took you through an open woods of red oaks, and then along the high bank of the river till you came in sight of his fine cabin right between the river and the lake that took his name. . . . Yes sir, many a sufferin' bunch of men have walked that path with their thoughts stuck on their own problems instead of the beauty that was all around them.

Sylvester married in 1934 and brought his new wife, Eartha, into the big cabin to keep house for Mr. Henderson:

I got after Eartha again and again to marry me, but she kept holdin' back. Even though she knew Mr. Henderson, had visited the house several times, still she'd never been around whites before. So she took her time decidin'.

But after we finally got married, he treated her like a daughter, and she took loving good care of him.

Eartha's first three children were born in that cabin, and all were given Henderson family first names.

By the early thirties when Sylvester married, the cycle of homestead farming in southwest Arkansas was already in retreat. The oil boom hit in the region in 1923 and continued for a decade. After the first discovery wells were brought in, local farm labor was used to build roads and bridges, dig the oil pits and ditches, transport timbers and construct the drilling rigs that spread across the countryside. Even before the Great Depression the five big farms near the Henderson place were in decline. Working the poor sandy soil was no match for the beckoning oil and sawmill towns. All the Hendersons' own children had left one of the best farms in the region to seek their fortunes in the city, leaving Sylvester to care for their father on the old homestead until he died in 1950 at age seventy-nine. Knowing that upon his death the Henderson heirs would sell the farm or bring in a white overseer, the old gentleman had advised Sylvester to leave the farm behind after his death and seek an independent living elsewhere to avoid humiliation or ill treatment at the hands of a white sharecropper. "The night the old man died, I dreamed on it and studied my situation over. I knew of a vacant house on Jelly Roll in Calion that I could rent. The next morning I had made my mind up to leave for good."

Then Sylvester gathered up his family, leaving behind his beloved farm, and started a new life as a sawmill hand in the bustling, sometimes raucous town of Calion just five miles away.

The family settled quickly into the Calion community. Well-liked and comfortable with his white employers, Sylvester established himself as a versatile and reliable employee at the mill. In the black community they were already known through the nearby Baptist Church at Champagnolle that was attended by a number of Jelly Roll blacks. As Sylvester aptly summarizes the move, "It wasn't far and it wasn't hard. Lotsa' good God-fearing brothers and sisters already in Jelly Roll. But Saturday night was a shock then, and it still is now when so many of these people here are workin' at destroying themselves."

When the old timers harken back to days gone by — of God-fearing men and women, honest hard work, and Christian fellowship — they are inclined to forget or underplay the violence and crimes of passion so frequent then in the Jelly Roll community. When they do recount the barroom brawls, knifings, and murders, it is usually with an indulgent shrug, part of "the old sawmill days," a time of tough living in crowded quarters, bootlegging, hard drinking and hard loving:

> Now the main street of Jelly Roll was a clean street. Everyone kept their homes up pretty and nice, nothin' like this old briar patch we're livin' in now. You could stand on your porch right here and see all the way to the railroad tracks, three trains north and three trains south every day, wide open with several lots for the kids to play baseball.
>
> The nicest people lived right here up and down this street. You might say they were the upper-class colored citizens, church people. Of course, back then the town was crowded, more people lived here then, but they also came pourin' in on Saturdays from all around. What made the biggest difference in those days here were beer joints and bootleg. . . . Drinkin', gamblin', and fightin', that was the rough side of the sawmill life. But now it has blessedly moved away to El Dorado, and you have to go to the lake to a beer joint. But when we first came to Calion, this was a town and a half. On weekends the dice were rollin', and the street swarmin'. People getting cut up was routine, and there were lots of shootings. It was a good town during the week, but on weekends if you hit the streets as a stranger, you'd better not go runnin' your mouth or they would hem you up and go to cuttin' on you. A man was stabbed to death, another killed with a .38 right dead center between the eyes. Well, back then the law took lightly to what was going on here. It took a big fight or a murder to see the sheriff; and even a murderer, if he was a good worker, could get himself paroled in no time. Old Bill West was the meanest one around. He had eyes like a snake. Dangerous! His eyes were always turnin', but he'd never look straight at you. He always said, 'Keep your eyes on a man's feet, and if they move wrong, kill him.' Old Bill didn't play around. He shot a man four times in Pine Bluff. Bill wasn't a college man, but he was a whiz with electricity, so the power company got him paroled for a while until he shot another man in the woods six times. Back in those days, violence was everyday news.

Although both Eartha and Sylvester made a seemingly easy adjustment to a new life in Calion, they did not delude themselves that it was by choice or for the best. A treasured quality of life had been left behind forever. God had spoken. They had complied. The effects upon their children, however, would, by their own admission, be far-reaching. Of seven, the first three were born on the farm. The first two were in their teens before the move. Sylvester concludes:

> You could see a change steady growing in the younger children. Why the oldest would run ahead of the car on Sunday to beat us to church. Later the younger ones wouldn't go if you carried them there.... Well, then, Eartha and I just didn't raise 'em the same in town. We'd say, 'No, you can't go out!' Then apologize for it. Or, I'd say, 'No,' and they'd go talk Eartha down.... On the farm there was no non-sense. We thought alike. They knew what they had to do, and town was far away.

Here, we hit upon a dominant theme: a lament over the loss of structure, meaning, and the disciplined life. It recurs in many forms in other interviews.

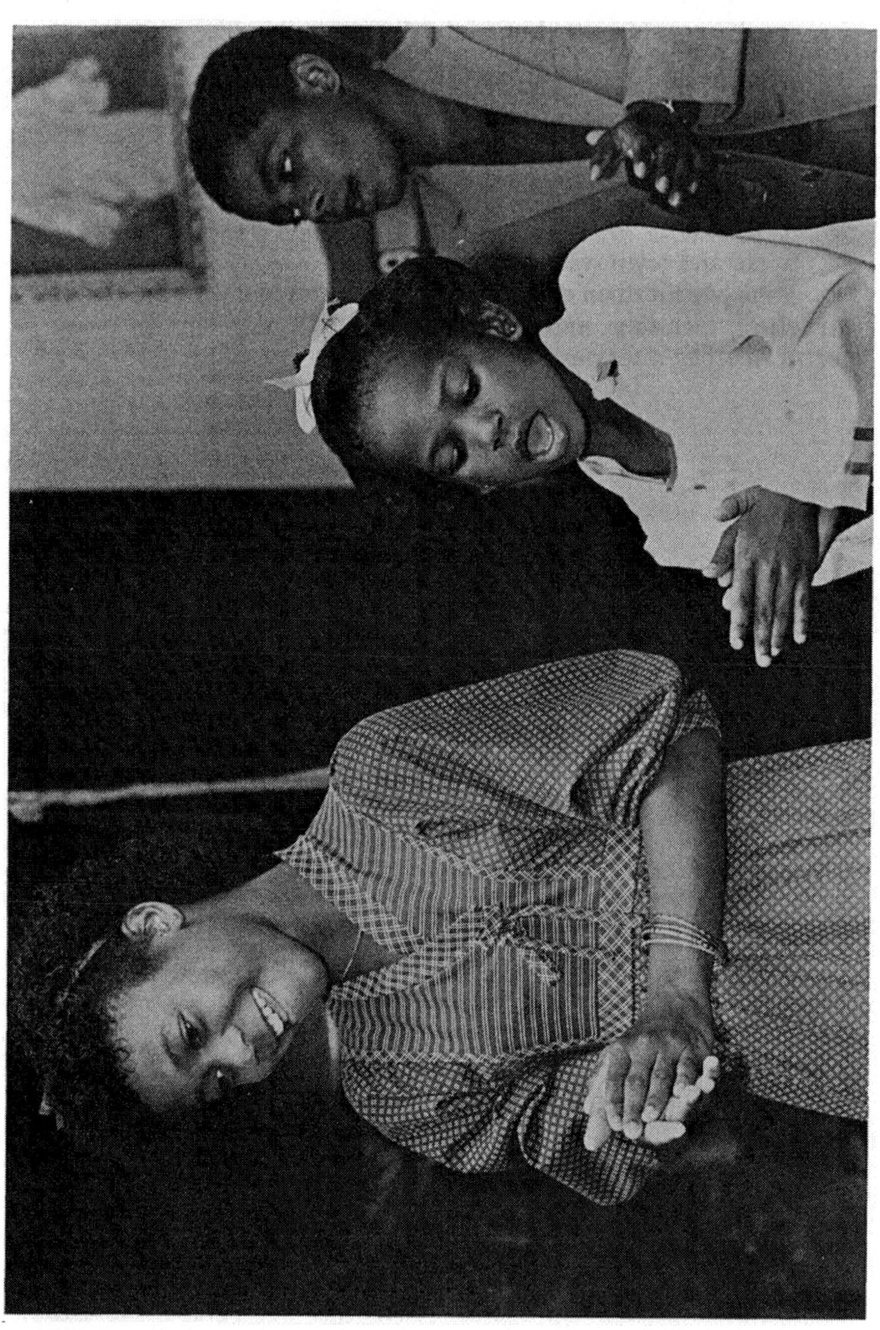

Singing to Jesus

CHAPTER 4

Hattie Jenkins

A Missionary of the Gospel

She is quite old, eighty-six, and she lives alone, an elderly widow; but her age is the only thing old about Hattie Jenkins. She is a tall woman, still erect, wears wire spectacles on an only slightly wrinkled face with high forehead and cheekbones. When she begins to speak, her age vanishes, so alert, curious, and full of life are her remarks and train of thought. She speaks with a cultured accent, a preacher's daughter with a high-pitched voice. She is never tentative in what she says and her thoughts reflect the security of her knowledge. Like the person, her house is neat but unadorned. The Bible, "my best friend and companion," showing the patina of constant use, rests on the table by her easy chair. With only one surviving child, a daughter who lives out of state, she has no other close relatives, but she is nonetheless a busy, involved woman, close to friends and church. In fact, I first met Miss Hattie when we were both visitors at the Johnson home. She had joined vigorously into an already heated discussion of child rearing and had the last word:

> Our children are being cheated today. They don't know what discipline is. They don't have to do anything. Not answerable for anything. But we were raised to get up and get out. And they're not strong in Jesus the way we were. Lord, how I remember the joy of getting ready to go to church. Not just on Sunday, I mean almost everyday. In

those days you didn't have to go inside to hear the praying! It came pourin' out the windows and through the doors. We couldn't wait to get to church, got in a trot to the door. And it wasn't just for show the way it is now, see and be seen. Yes, we ironed and ironed on that one white dress, put lard on our shoes to make 'em shine. But we were there in Jesus, praising His name and learning His lessons.

Hattie Jenkins' thorough religious education is central to her character and speech. Largely self-taught with only a grammar school education, she was always eager to engage in Biblical discussions or disputations for, "The Bible says we're supposed to keep Jesus first in our minds and hearts."

Miss Hattie came to Calion as a young bride almost sixty years ago. She married Henry Jenkins, a lumber stacker from the nearby sawmill town of Wesson. They were married for fifty-six years before his death, had two daughters, only one still living, along with six grandchildren, all of whom live in Texarkana.

For most of us there is a natural tendency in old age to become more withdrawn, to cling to family and familiar things, and let the rest go by. In Calion the retired and aged are, as a group, inveterate porch sitters, watching the trucks roll by to and from the mill, waving or nodding to the town as they frequently wheel and walk past. Increasingly detached from the world around them, the old folks take their ease after a life of hard physical labor, letting their present immobility announce to the world that they are getting a long-deserved rest. But while a majority of the town's elders quietly vegetate, Miss Hattie can be seen in the cool of the morning briskly walking the streets on her daily round of visitations to the shut-ins. "I have my mission. Jesus says to help those that can't help themselves, and I still have many old friends in Calion that can't get about much anymore. Jesus walked everywhere doin' good; He didn't ride, you know."

Miss Hattie, like so many of her age, has warm memories from the Great Depression in this little community. She remembers the united efforts of the local churches to care for the needy and the organized group activities to raise money, like picking blackberries and selling them along the highway. In reflecting on the passing parade of years in the same little town she is more concerned about the declining influence of the Church, the Word, and the Christian spirit:

People today are as easy as popcorn. They tell you one thing and do another. They follow the crowd no matter where it carries them. They're doin' everything but the right thing. Jesus says that no one can live your life for you, no one is going to die for you; for Jesus is coming back for your life, not a Sunday meeting! He said, 'Go unto your closet and pray, and I will open you wider.' That doesn't mean go shouting in church and think it is prayer — shiny shoes and loud voices. Jesus said we would be known by our works, but now the church seems to be helping everyone but those that need it; and sayin' who should come in the door and who should stay out. Now Jesus wanted us all out in the world, 'The field is wide and the laborers few,' he said. . . . I believe like old Pop, who burned up in his house not long ago; he lived right by the church but never went in. Some people say that's why he burned, but I say you can be a good Christian and never cross the church house door. The real church is in your heart. Jesus said you would be known by the fruit you bear. You have to do good before you get your crown.

Throughout her long and virgorous life, Miss Hattie has been prominent in her community. She is greeted warmly everywhere by young and old. Her strength belies her years, and her faith provides the constant impetus and direction to her life and at an age when most have succumbed to lethargy and a narrowing routine.

Her life was never easy. Henry Jenkins was always a common laborer, and in less prosperous times Miss Hattie had to "work out" in order to raise a family and own a home. She worked as a housekeeper for various prominent families in El Dorado over many years, following her husband into retirement when they were both in their sixties. Her long association with wealthy whites seems to have affected her little; from her recollections she appears to have found these associations neither humiliating nor uplifting, simply part of a job to be done:

Jesus said we are made of the same blood. I never resented what white people had. We all have the privilege to enjoy the really good things in life, but I have seen many abuse this privilege. I've seen them sit at the table and eat so much they'd have to be carried to the doctor. In Timothy Jesus said, 'I believe that everything God made is good or very good.' But you can even drink too much water, and we know that water is good for everyone. No, I never coveted what white folks had, so I stayed in good humor most of the time, didn't get humped up over wanting what I didn't have or couldn't ever have.

Right after we were first married, I told Henry I wanted a home of my own and a decent living is all I asked. People today work and work to get fine homes, but then they stay too much in them. I have a nice common place. It's comfortable but I'm not crazy about it. If I get a call from a neighbor or my daughter in Texarkana, I'm gone in a minute.

She raised two daughters in the strict traditional mold of "church, school, and more church." She was devoted to the belief that training is all, and that you "set an example and it spreads around the house; and the best thing you can give your children is advice." Even at eighty-six, Miss Hattie sees the troubles and corruptions of youth today as resting on the doorstep of the older generation:

> We're responsible for their sins. We dopefied them with the sorry ways we have come to live ourselves. We sin openly in front of our children. We've lost our own respectability; so how can we expect the blind to lead the blind? The kids today have no future. These low types will pay you no mind, and see no example worthy of following. . . . I was raised in a peaceful, quiet home. I don't understand the craziness going on all around us. But, then, like Jesus said, we live in the middle of sin, not above it.

The only apparent major trauma in Miss Hattie's long tranquil life was the violent death of her younger daughter a decade ago. She was killed in Texarkana in a bizarre incident, stabbed to death while standing in line at a cafeteria. As her mother related it in the sparsest terms, "My daughter, Ellen, caught the lick that was intended for someone else. The stab killed her, and that's about all they told me about it." Invariably, when questioned further, she falls silent at this point, and only later added:

> I let the rest of the family handle all the burial things. They put her away in pink: pink dress, pink ribbons and flowers, even a pink coffin. It was lovely and all that, but they've gone too far with finery. Anyway, give me flowers while I'm still livin'.

It is one of the few subjects that Hattie Jenkins will not discuss freely, an inner blow covered over many years ago. With distant eyes she concludes, "Jesus said that he wouldn't put on us more than we could bear." Sometimes she appears like this, infinitely remote from the contemporary world, even the tragic death of her own daughter. There is an aura of spirituality about her, the reflection of intense convictions, a remnant from a time when the endurance of physical hardship and disappointment was a common phenomenon to be borne with the aid of God and the Word. Self-taught beyond a grammar-school education, Miss Hattie reflects the American black culture that from slave days to the present has eloquently expressed its deep and abiding faith in the next world as well as resignation to the burdens placed upon them in this life.

CHAPTER 5

Willie and Babe Cole

Coping with Poverty

The residence of Willie Cole stands out from the row of vintage prefabs only by virtue of its relative neglect. "That house shows all the signs of disinterest," says a neighbor. During an extended period of prosperity and labor shortages in the mid-Fifties the company built this block-long model of middle-class suburbia, an innovation for its time never before anticipated by the local black community. Sold to employees for $100 down, 3% interest, and a $6 per week payroll deduction plan, the project was a great success, as new and old employees alike vied for the privilege of owning a home with modern kitchen and bathroom.

Willie Cole made the most eligible employee list hands down. A six-foot-four strapping big man in the prime of his forties, Willie commanded respect from blacks and whites alike as an unslacking, ever-reliable worker. Combining muscle and humor to the delight of fellow workers, he was always the first with his hands to move the heaviest railroad ties or lumber; and since he always carried more than his share, he was never at a loss for friends.

In many respects Willie typified much of the rural black labor force in the Fifties, working sometimes for years on end without a layoff, ever in tune with the white bosses' needs, a part of a versatile crew that was equally competent at stoking boilers, handling heavy timbers, or fine-tuning an old gasoline engined tractor. Typically unschooled beyond the third grade and familiar with only the county in which he grew up, Willie was reconciled to a lifetime of hard physical labor; and hard work was just a necessity of poverty, not a road to salvation. With a mind and body trained to unfailing answer of the six o'clock morning whistle five days a week, he could on weekends plunge whole-heartedly into life's most basic gratifications; for neither hardship nor personal troubles long darkened his personality and wit.

He was born in small quarters to a mother unconcerned about another child and was taught early the virtues of silence and inconspicuousness at home, finding out at an early age that happiness was immersion in the crowd. As Willie says about his youth, "When I was little, nobody over took my picture." As part of a large family in cramped quarters, he quickly evolved a street personality: "I hate the inside, only cold and rain gonna keep me in," as he puts it. Today in retirement Willie spends most of his time out-of-doors sitting on the edge of his porch with his feet dangling. Here he takes two meals a day much of the the year; and when it's raining or very cold, he likes to sit at the wheel of his derelict pickup truck, abandoned at the side of the house. There, out of the elements, in winter bundled up against the cold, he sits "watchin' the folks," happily waving and greeting all passers-by. His wife, Babe, gives him his allotment of wine and he watches his world, sometimes solemnly through distant eyes, but always there.

At just sixty-eight, Willie is now an old man in rapid physical decline. Overweight, tottering now on legs swollen with old injuries and bad circulation, a growing, ever-shifting belly as prominent as his snow white hair, "Papa Cole" has become the affectionate symbol of the good life that elderly blacks enjoyed only after retirement.

By the standards of an achieving society, Willie's career has been anything but a success; but in many basic ways he has succeeded: in his hard labor, his jovial role in the community, and by providing a good home and fathership to his common-law wife and her many children. All of this despite the fact that Willie was, sociologically speaking, "downwardly mobile." The son of a railroad worker, he never rose above the entry level job his father had obtained for him on a Missouri-Pacific track gang, a job given probably because of bad times, racial discrimination in promotion, and Willie's outward passivity. In time, he quit "the Line" in search of less physical demanding labor. Since the choices were limited, he gravitated toward sawmilling, and after a few jobs, a few layoffs (he has reverently kept all the discharge and unemployment slips covering his working career in an old cigar box), in his thirties he settled down at Calion, getting his first job with the company repairing their railroad switch track. Later he transferred to the sawmill and finally the lumberyard where after a lifetime of hard work he retired as a common laborer earning less, relatively speaking, at the end of his career than at its beginning. However, thirty years with the company had at least earned him the good house which was strategic to his future life and reputation.

Willie struggled with a long-term love affair with a woman of the streets. Mable Jackson, or Babe as she was affectionately known to both her black and white clients, became in her prime his lifelong love, his off-again, on-again consort, the mother of his and other children he housed, fed and clothed. Ultimately she became the consolation of his old age.

Babe was a child of hard times and a broken home. Born in 1925, she spent her childhood and early youth under the stigma of being black and impoverished during the Great Depression. Her story is best summarized in her own words:

> We lived in Calion in this old rent house, my mother, auntie, Granny, li'l brother and me. I was a fool over my mama but she died givin' birth to my sister right here in the house. Last thing she said, 'Sister, take care of your little brother'; then she raised her hand to wave at the angels in heaven.
>
> I was left with Auntie then; she married a man named Smith, and he moved in with us. Auntie never liked me, but after Mama died she took a terrible dislike to me — once threw all my clothes, shoes 'n everything out in the rain. Half the time she wouldn't feed me. Granny hid food for us children to have some poor sumptin' to eat. Even when food was short Granny made me light a fire in the stove so as neighbors think we was cookin' supper! Yeah, I remember my childhood all right. Not enough a nothin' is hard to forget!

If a common response to poverty's despair is resignation and alcohol, Babe's was the opposite: work, determination and moderation. Even in the hardest of times this formula produced results; for Babe had both the will and an advantage, an apparently irresistible attractiveness to men, black and white. Using all the pubescent charm of a fourteen-year-old, she landed a much-sought-after job in 1938 as a waitress in an uptown cafe at $1.50 per day and initiated a winning formula by bestowing her after-hours favors on her customers. "I got my first baby in the back seat of a cab takin' me home from work," she laughs. Fourteen is a tender age for making life decisions, but Babe made hers without hesitation, recognizing the economic advantages, accepting the implications of her actions without delusion or fear. She embraced the strife and resentment that her professional biracial connections would entail. Moving eagerly to capitalize on her natural talents, she extricated herself from the grinding poverty that was her peers' ordinary fate. Babe was successfully coping and would continue to do so until age foreclosed her career.

But life was not easy. Always on her own when the chips were down, forever stared at with lustful disrespect by men, harassed sometimes openly, but more often in cutting little ways by other women, a revolving door passing men through her life, it was in the final analysis, a lonely and sometimes sordid business. Babe speaks with disconcerting calm about being gang raped by four white men after leaving the cafe one night, of walking down the highway and being forced into a truck to have sex with its driver, and of slipping across the river at dusk to meet the "clap doctor" who gave her treatment when she caught a disease. Moreover, in a "two-bit town like this'n," her profits were modest; and as the babies came with inadequate birth control, so did the bills and complications. Between the ages of nineteen and thirty-five she bore eight children, three boys, only one of whom finished high school and got a good job. The other two "were sorta plain and never amounted to much."

All five of the girls, on the other hand, bore, despite their diverse paternity, the stamp of their mother's beauty and style. "All my children were handsome because I didn't mess with no ugly men; well, 'cept after dark for money when you couldn't see 'em anyhow," Babe relates with an amused laugh. If her boys grew up aimlessly without parental direction, the girls fell naturally into their mother's regime. Under her tutelage and ever watchful eye they were groomed before puberty for eventually joining her enterprise. Two of the girls, Cindy and Barbara, completed high school, went on to obtain well-paid jobs, marry and raise their own families, and for reasons never clearly stated by suggesting that their superior academic abilities provided them with other alternatives, avoided their mother's trafficking with men. Two other girls accepted their mother's arrangements during their teenage years before marrying and moving out; but Clara, the middle daughter, closest to her mother in appearance and temperament, became her protege and partner before she was shot to death at just nineteen.

Clara's tragic murder came to rest at Babe's feet, for she had been in every way her mother's child; "she could throw her thing and stop the traffic," dating men of her mother's choosing from her early teens. Unfortunately she lacked her mother's aptitude for diplomacy, being instead hot-tempered and impetuous to a degree that became her undoing.

She married short of sixteen, pregnant by the boy across the street, Terry Boone, and soon gave birth to a beautiful, wide-eyed daughter whom she named Christine. Babe says their marriage was good, a love match from the start, but that Clara's mother-in-law, Hattie Boone, disapproving and jealous of the match, succeeded in destroying her son's love from within while tempting him with other women from without.

Babe describes a raucous night of heavy drinking not long before their divorce: with a group of boisterous friends, Terry, fondling another woman, had stood on the porch at his mother's house, while Clara, barely constrained by her mother, stood in the street brandishing a loaded revolver, cursing and screaming threats at her infidel husband and his "hussy." The third and last year they were married was one of growing estrangement. Clara was dating Sam Nobles, "a bright-skinned man, sometimes mistook for white," whom she later married and with whom she moved to Magnolia immediately after her divorce from Terry. But once again the spector of violent exploitative relationships emerged; and within a matter of a few months after her marriage to Sam, Clara was visited at her new home by her mother who was shocked to find her "beat up and limp as a rag doll. That man had the habit of chokin' her till she passed out. Mean! Somethin' funny about him. Treated her mostly like a bad child. They had some terrible fights, and he fought tough."

Nonetheless, Clara gave birth to a healthy baby boy and within months, while he lay in his crib, Clara was found shot to death in her bed. Husband Sam first confessed to murder and was jailed, but later pleaded innocent and amidst much indifferent legal procrastination was set free and never prosecuted.

Throughout this violent and sordid affair Babe herself suffered much criticism and blame from the community. Many claimed that she had continued to encourage, if not arrange, Clara's encounters with other men during both her marriages. To these charges Babe holds herself blameless, at least publicly, and in several long conversations on the subject produced endless plots and counterplots that failed to clarify or resolve the tragic event which left an infant grandson and three-year-old granddaughter for her to raise. For as often occurs in Jelly Roll, the fathers of both children "took out," refusing custody or support, choosing wisely in terms of their pocketbooks if not their duty to let welfare assume their support and grandmother their guardianship from infancy to adulthood.

Babe and Willie took the infant and young girl into their home where they have lived for the last eight years, drawing at this writing from the Aid to Families With Dependent Children program $172 per month and $142 in food stamps plus free medical care. In a classic case of indifferent administration, two fathers in two legal marriages, both good job-holders, have gone free of financial obligation to care for their offspring.

Although this case may represent a dereliction of duty on the part of the welfare authorities, it has been much to the good of the two children. Clara's life style had left two antagonistic fathers who would probably have been poor providers and little comfort to their children, while a secure welfare income provided them with welcome entry into Babe's home where they have received an affectionate and concerned upbringing for the last eight years.

The years following Willie's move into the good prefab house in 1958, when he had bested all his rivals for Babe's true affections, were good years for him, a time of peace and prosperity whose trickledown effects at least insured him of a steady job at the mill with annually increasing pay. The year after their move, Babe gave birth to the only child by him, Shirley Jean. Although he showed her many little signs of special affection, Willie loved all his girls and the attention they so generously bestowed upon him as titular father and head of the household. How well I can myself remember little Shirley Jean and her older sister, Clara, standing every Friday at the sawmill gate waiting for the noon whistle to escort "Poppa" directly home for dinner and collect his paycheck without a detour to the liquor store. Willie seemed forever content to be his women's pawn, and as the years slipped by and his daughters became teenagers, Willie found himself presiding over the comings and goings of suitors and clients alike, a good-natured impresario for his household of girls.

However, he apparently sustained a light-hearted wit only by turning a blind eye to his own inner conflicts. Babe knew that Willie was filled with jealousy and resentment toward the men who crowded his premises, and so he drank. And when he drank he physically abused them all except his own Shirley Jean, always saving the heaviest hand for Babe. "That man got so he'd jump me every day at noon — come in the house and straight way choke me and kick me all the while accusin' me of things. I had to stick him with an ice pick or butcher knife, tryin' not to cut too deep. Got so bad I just set on the butcher knife all the time for when he came near. Finally I just fill up a big ol' paper sack of my things, gathered up my girls and moved to Rock Island (a district in El Dorado, some twelve miles away)."

The year following Babe's departure, Clara was murdered. Meanwhile the resilient Babe had rented an old house uptown and Willie was left alone in Calion. These years apart were hard times for him without even so much as one daughter left to bring him a hot meal from time to time. Alone, unfed, and uncared for, he succumbed to depression and alcohol; sitting morosely on the porch steps staring at the ground, he ignored the passing parade of friends and neighbors. As in the old days when the girls met him at the gate on payday, so now he saw his family mostly on Fridays when Babe came out with some food and to help cash his check.

When he had first been left alone there had been a flurry of active empathy by friends and neighbors. Folks came to commiserate, some bearing cornbread and a pot of greens. One of his girls would occasionally spend the night, or stay long enough at least to straighten up the growing clutter in his bachelor's warren. But in Jelly Roll, overriding the limited goodwill and mutuality between neighbors, is an ever-present suspicion of foul play and the fear of being sucked into the turbulence that surrounded other people's lives. To compound the problem, with his paycheck pilfered every Friday, overrunning his credit limit at the grocery, and always in need of another beer, Willie began to borrow money wherever he could, thereby alienating himself from those few friends that were left. In this miserable state, in steadily declining health, he wore out the better part of six years.

At last, in 1979 Babe returned, now white-haired with only one unmarried daughter, Shirley Jean, and Clara's two orphaned children. Once more Willie and Babe were reconciled, together again to share their declining years, and once more Papa Willie's house rang out with his laughter as of days gone by.

A year after this study was completed Papa Willie had a major stroke that left him crippled in mind and body. He recovered enough to use a walker in the house, but thereafter the household was sobered by the constant care that his declining condition demanded.

When I arrived late one cold January afternoon, I found that the children had both been home from school all day with various complaints and, consequently, Babe was in one of her highstrung moods. The following dialogue transpired:

> Babe: "Oh, Oh! Sometimes I think I'm chokin' to death in this place. Can't catch my breath. Got nowhere to go and no money to get there. I'm too old for these children! Allen up all night cryin' with a toothache. Christine wanderin' the house complainin' with cramps in her leg. Willie settin' on the edge of his bed talkin' to his self the whole night long. You think I slept a wink? I give it up and sat on this couch watchin' the street all night. What's going on out there? Honey, you'd be surprised. Folks sneakin' out and folks sneakin' in. Alma out looking for a man, any man, honey!

Golden years of retirement

George and Henry prowlin' the streets looking for a game or a drink. Truck drivers leavin' out. This street don't never sleep."

Allen: "Momma, I'm hungry. My stomach's growlin'. Can I have three dollars to go to Joe B's for a hamburger!"

Babe: "What you talk, boy! I got no three dollars for Joe B's. An you don't need to be out in the cold air with a bad tooth. I'll fix somethin' in a little while. Just steady down. Christine, give him one of those honey buns over there."

Christine: "Ain't none. We ate the last, and we're about out of soda, too."

Babe: "Got to go to town for fresh supplies when we take you to the doctor tomorrow. I haven't been to the grocery in almost a week. Don't care about sellin' nothin'. Been in one of my don't-give-a-damn moods. I'm worried about Christine's leg. That old doctor she been going to keep sayin' the hurtin' in her leg is muscles, but I know it's worse than that. It goes numb, and that ain't muscles. I'm afraid it's from the heart fever she had when she was little. She has to take medicine until she's twenty-one he says, so it won't come back on her."

Christine: "I had to give up the high school basketball team, and that broke my heart, but I was hurtin' too bad."

Babe: "Don't you think she ought to have a government disability? We need the money, but that old doctor just nods his head and looks at the ground sayin' she'll be all right if she takes her medicine. What's it to him if she gets a disability. He just nods his head and won't sign nothin'. White folks is naturally stingy. I think you know it [laughs]."

Christine: "Momma, why do you have to make everything white or black?"

Babe: "When you lived as long as me maybe it'll come to you. Oh, I'm short today. Truth be, I had a fight last night with Donald [her son] and his girlfriend. They're tryin' to move in on me, but I told 'em plain, I'm not gonna have it. Donald got a wife and a home he never goes to. His girlfriend got a good [welfare] check, but she keep her kids with her mother. I've never seen Donald so close by a girl before. Never. He must love this one the way he be watchin' her all the time. But the money's messed up. Her mama got the kids and the check, and you know Donald don't stay long on a job. The two of them were asleep on the couch here last night at 3 a.m. Then I put 'em out. He's my own, but he'll take anything you got. Go to missin' towels, soap, even. An the refrigerator is empty. What else can I do? Do you blame me? Since Papa Willie had his stroke he's useless. I've got to tend to him and raise these kids by myself. I've got my ways — what's right, what's not. These kids don't need to be seein'

Donald and that girl humpin' on the couch. . . . I told him he ought to go back to his old lady, but he just stare at me."

Christine: "Donald's in love, Mama. You not gonna change that."

Babe: "Donald gonna do what he gonna do, but not here. I made it plain. Now he's mad. Didn't show up to take me and Allen to the dentist today. I had to pay a neighbor six dollars to drive us. And Christine wouldn't go to the doctor because she wouldn't leave Papa Willie alone."

Willie: "I told you, don't worry 'bout me. Don't worry 'bout me all the time."

Babe: "Just be quiet, Willie. We're talkin' over here. . . . He don't make no sense. His mind about gone. Sometimes I just sit here and cry to myself. What can I do? I know what I gotta do. I've got to hang in there. Take care of this old man of mine and these kids as best I can. Nobody's comin' by to take up my load. My own boy charges me six dollars to drive me up town. Neighbors quit comin' to see Papa Willie."

Christine: "What about Norma Jean [one of Babe's daughters]? She helps out all the time."

Babe: "Wouldn't take a million for her, either. She's so sweet and thoughtful. Buys things for the kids and me whenever she's able. No, I wouldn't take nothin' for her, I'll tell you. Well, now I'm gonna wash Papa Willie up and fix us all some supper. It's been a sorry day."

CHAPTER 6

Erma and Jefferson Bates

Pillars of the Church

Just across the tracks from Mill Street, which is the "Main Street" of Jelly Roll, is the quiet pine tree glade where black-topped lanes wind past a dozen houses isolated from the rest of the black community. This area affords a cozy retreat from the hurly-burly of Mill Street, an alternative life-style for those who want some distance between them and the brasher elements of street life, the continual scrutiny of neighbors, and close living quarters. This wooded sector of town seems a perfect setting for Erma and Jefferson Bates, an elderly, reserved couple whose quiet dignity infuses all that surrounds them. Their modest but trim frame house adjoins a large vegetable garden. Everything at this residence, like the carefully laid-out rows of vegetables, is orderly and well cared for. The inside of their home evokes an air of middle-class graciousness and comfort. Carpeting is wall to wall, freshly laundered curtains adorn all the windows, the overstuffed furniture in the living room is color coordinated, a handsome dining room suite fills the adjoining room, and beyond in the master bedroom there is an obviously valuable antique fourposter bed.

Erma Bates, sixty-four, has all the quiet poise and dignity that one usually associates with class. In fact, she promptly informed me that she was a poor minister's daughter, that her father had once been the pastor of Jelly Roll's large Willow Grove Baptist Church.

Mrs. Bates has worked as a servant for a wealthy and prominent El Dorado family for the last twenty-seven years. It is her white family's castoff antiques that add distinction and an aura of elegance to the Bates' little home. "The lady has always been lovely to me," she notes with feeling for her employer of so many years.

Erma Bates received a grammar-school education from a segregated country school; but her language, vocabulary, and general demeanor suggest much more, possibly the influence of her pastor father's world and the upper-class white household to which she has devoted so many years as a domestic servant. She regrets never having had any children but has committed her leisure time to the Sunday School of the Willow Grove Church.

Jefferson Bates is seventy-two, but in every way appears to be at least ten years younger. His hair remains black with only a few flecks of gray. He is lean, erect, clear-eyed, a vigorous outdoorsman who proudly cultivates a big vegetable garden in the old Jelly Roll tradition. Church and garden are obviously his greatest joys. Mr. Bates, although well up in years and retired from the furniture plant, continued to work there in the summers "to pick up some spare change" until he was seventy:

> I started work for Calion Lumber Co. walking stacks [as a lumber handler] in 1946 when I came out of service. Of course, first I got hitched to this old girl here, and that gave me a good reason to find some steady work. I married Erma on Friday the thirteenth, and that's been my lucky number all my life. We've been married thirty-seven years, I never believed I'd be with the same woman for that long. Now, I guess we're just gonna wear out together. We've had a good life, we've seen a lot of improvements in this town. Do you remember how it used to stink before we got sewers and water? Folks would be dumpin' in one hole and drinkin' out of another. . . . Work! Man, we had work down on that lumberyard pullin' those big wide boards off the green chain onto those old iron-wheeled wagons. Bust your guts is what it would do! I got myself transferred to the furniture plant. Up there a man can still be old and work. It's lighter. [Now] sawmilling is not as rough as it used to be. More push-button boys, lift trucks instead of contrary mules. . . . This job has come a long way since I was a young man out there.

Jefferson Bates is a traditionalist. A man who believes that what was right in the past should still be right, and so observed, in the present. He has long been a pillar of the Willow Grove Baptist Church and vigorously continues to oppose the quickening tide of modern permissiveness. Through his somewhat aloof authoritarian attitudes, he and his wife, who is superintendent of the Sunday School, have attempted to maintain and "sanctify" traditional standards of piety, duty, and respect among the youth of their church. As Jefferson puts it, "When I approach them, the young people will likely grow quiet." Is his role too much to be tolerated in a permissive age? Apparently the faithful remain, although their numbers diminish. Jefferson fights a continuous battle against peer-group pressure, the other side. "I tell them all, don't be what the streets want, be what you want to be." The message is heeded by the faithful and the strong, but for many of Jelly Roll's youth, "the church is not where I'm at or where I'm coming from."

Erma Bates, herself childless, laments the painful generation gap she experiences in her church work:

> I've been at Willow Grove since I was born. I hate to see empty pews. I wish other people would come in and join us; we have such a fine pastor, now. People have lost respect for the Church. They don't think about God. We live like in Noah's day with evil everywhere. When somebody dies we fill up the church but the rest of the time we are just the regulars. . . . Our parents kept to basics. If you went to a ball game you went to church first. [Parents] today ask their kids instead of tell them. Children in the twelth grade can't read and write as I can even though I only went through the ninth grade, county schools at that! I don't know whether the schools can't teach or the children can't learn. When they read their Bible out loud it sounds flat, doesn't mean anything to them. . . . The kids have no responsibilities, not to their parents, not to themselves.

Jefferson breaks in:

> Won't even take care of number one. Sundown comes but nobody knows where they are — not at home, roamin' the streets. We had our daily chores. I carried water, God knows how far. I lost my mother when I was nine. Never saw my daddy. I quit the fourth grade to go scratchin' around to support my five brothers and sisters. We had it tough, but we didn't complain. . . .

Mrs. Bates continues her side of the story:

> When I started to work as a maid here in Calion in 1942, I made three dollars a week, and that was for six days. Think of it! We moved to Detroit for two years where I made twenty dollars a week and thought I was rich. When Papa moved back home, I went to work in El Dorado where I could make five dollars. I'm still there, but I want for nothing. The Bible says we should be content with what we have. . . . Kids today refuse to live by their Bible. They

promise but they don't deliver. Church should be the first meaning in their lives, not the last. Everything, everywhere yields to money — our political and spiritual structure. We need to go back to the backbone like they say.

Jefferson being obviously of similar mind joined vigorously in the discussion:

> In the old days there were two kinds of folks in Jelly Roll. Nice folks, the church folks and law-abiding citizens, were one group, and the outlaws were the other. The rascally bunch were a class to themselves. It was as simple as that. If a young girl got pregnant they made her drop out of school so she couldn't mix with the girls that didn't. If you didn't want to make something of yourself, then move them shoes! Now people just gather you in. No matter what you do they gonna treat you nice. Now the good folks and the bad folds is all mixed up together and good and bad is forgotten.

Erma concludes on a similar note:

> Our people have always said, 'if only the black people just had a chance, what they could do! Now they got their chance and they're squandering it. . . . They want it all. They want the best jobs, but won't prepare or sacrifice to get them. The opportunity is there, one we never had, and they're letting it slip by them. . . . I think everything is too convenient now. The water is in the house. No wood to chop. Come in after school, throw your books down and be gone on the streets.

Undoubtedly we have encountered here a time-honored tradition in which the older generation vents its disillusionment and despair over the deplorable state of youth. However, in Jelly Roll this familiar lament seems particularly pertinent. The older generation is both bitter and deeply disturbed by so much that they see around them.

CHAPTER 7

Odelia Jackson

Alone in the Neighborhood

The Jackson house is painted a vivid pink and stands alone on a spacious lot facing the main highway through Calion. Although it is no more than 200 feet from the row of houses on Thomas Street, it is widely viewed as isolated, unnaturally positioned ("like white folks houses"), and far too big for a widow. In short, the house has become a symbol of what is regarded around town as Miss Odelia's uniqueness and anti-social behavior.

Odelia Jackson is a spry eighty-two, a widow whose husband, Herbert, was one of the original crew that started up the mill in the 1920s. She had only two children, boys; the younger died in 1933 at age seven while the older, Barry, grew up to become, despite three failed marriages of his own, his mother's constant companion and the solace of her widowed years. Barry Jackson, like his father, worked at the mill until a year ago when, at the age of fifty-seven on a hot Saturday afternoon in July, he was found dead of a heart attack that seized him while working under his car.

Miss Odelia is in every respect a member of the old guard. The daughter of a school teacher, largely self-taught but better educated than most blacks in the community, she is piously devoted and committed, even at eighty-two, to the work ethic. Everything around her shows a thoughtful hand, from the precise rows of asparagus and potatoes in her ample garden, to the neat what-not shelves in her living room that display her own handicraft. Her home is a visual reinforcement of her first words to me: "I was raised to work, I live to work, and all my life I have lived in that joy, and never suffered for want of anything."

Miss Odelia is an unusually tall woman, lean from a life of constant activity. Her short white hair is combed back casually, and her general appearance belies her age except for her squinting eyes and heavy spectacles worn to counteract developing cataracts. Seated in front of an assortment of oscillating fans in the living room on a hot, thundery afternoon she precisely recalled her younger days in Calion:

> Barry was born in '23 and we moved to Calion in '25. We arrived by buckboard wagon and mule and my husband, Herbert, went right to work at the mill leaving me with the house to move into. But in those days everyone pitched in to help, not like it is now where people would leave you to die in the streets! There weren't any cars in Calion 'cept for a few white folks in those days, and the roads were bad and we never went anywhere. But since nobody came to Calion or left it, the fishing was real good, so that's what we spent out spare time doing. Many an evening, I can remember at sundown seeing two men walking home with a long pole between them that held up long stringers of fish. Fishing is the only time I can be still. Mayor Epps used to let me use his boat on the lake where you could fish on either side, in the sun or in the shade. Happy memories.
>
> Now you may think it strange, but I have good memories of living here in the Depression. We didn't have any money, didn't work regular, we were deep in debt, owed fifty-four dollars at one time at the company commissary even though we only bought sugar, meal and salt. When Herbert worked at all he made ten cents an hour; and when the whistle blew on the sugar boat as it came up the river, people would jump out of the door and plain run to the dock for those ten-cent jobs unloading sugar and loading cotton. Many colored women went to work for white families as maids or cooks for a few pennies a day and scraps from the table that you wouldn't feed a dog. Fortunately, I never had to do that. I kept a big garden and, though it wasn't legal, I sold a whole string of bream or white perch to white men from town for fifty cents. Sometimes I'd pick cotton for thirty-five cents a pound, but it got me in the knees so bad. Then Herbert would borrow the company mule to plow some white man's garden for fifty cents. Well, that's how we lived in the Hoover days. Just enough money to buy the few things you couldn't make. Of course, there were no

conveniences. Nothin' fancy. We had no experience with the modern way of life. I thought ice was just something that happened in winter. We pumped our wash water up the night before, it took so long to get a tub full. In winter, we lived mostly on turnips and sweet potatoes. Herbert raised hogs on swill made from garbage and dishwater, and we ate fresh fish and an occasional chicken. All that without seein' a dollar bill all together at one time. . .

I remember it was in the late '30s when Herbert finally got out of debt at the commissary and got six dollars cash money for his wages. Why we thought we'd struck it rich! Celebrated by goin' to town to spend it. But what stays in my sweet memory about those days was the way the colored cooperated with one another in everything and every way. There's strife now, but when times were hard people were more honorable instead of letting their selfish nature get the best of them. Now the colored are divided, stealing from each other and the white man, more mixing of the races. I never cared to mix except in business matters. All I ever wanted from the white man was justice, the same pay, justice in the court. Mixing the races is not necessary. In church I have noticed how different our voices are from whites. The songs we sing are different. Take the birds. They all drink at the same pond but otherwise stay to themselves.

Until about three years ago Miss Odelia and her son Barry lived on Mill Street, not far from the Willow Grove Baptist Church which they attended regularly. But they always felt that they were hemmed in "like the insides of a sandwich." They wanted a bigger garden, more space to move around, so they moved from the busy block and a short distance from street society where they had been accepted if not loved as somewhat eccentric and aloof. The move ruptured the already strained relations between them and some of their neighbors. The town's reaction turned hostile, and Miss Odelia says with barely suppressed emotion, "Some of my race acted outrageous, though I hate to talk against the colored, no one can be quite so hateful. They even threatened to burn our house down."

To add to her isolation Miss Odelia is seldom seen at church any more, claiming that her poor eyesight makes it difficult for her to walk the greater distance from her new home. But her personal alienation culminated with the experiences surrounding Barry's sudden death two years ago:

I'm still shaken with the loss of my boy. I can't get over it, can't get used to it. Barry was a parent-loving child from his first day. He was always such a good boy. Only time he

> ever got arrested was for speeding and he paid a thirty-eight dollar fine.
>
> We both liked the same things. We were 'stay at homes' and minded our own business, but many people hated us because of what we had. Secret envy! We weren't rich, just good managers. Now people want to steal what we have. . . . Somebody took five watermelons last night. Why didn't they ask? I would have given them to them. But the whole world is crime and evil-doing now. It's the fashion. The scriptures say not to do evil for evil. Can't be a Christian and hate. But I think on it sometimes. Can you believe it that some people are telling each other what they're going to take from this house when I die? There's talk of buried money here and all such nonsense. . . . I don't have a relative in Union County. When Barry died they passed right by without a sign, no card, no flowers. I sat alone in the funeral home waiting for all those neighbors to come. . . . The Lord prophesied that before the Judgement Day it would be man against man.

Within weeks of this interview, Miss Odelia was badly beaten by her grandson who shortly before had come from California to live with her. Her hopes for companionship and solace in her old age were shattered when, through threats of violence, he made her a prisoner in her own home. Apparently she was too frightened and too slow to escape from the house for help. He was a young man, twenty-five or so, an ex-convict on parole from the California prison sytem, a quiet young man who Miss Odelia says had been poisoned with hatred by his mother after she divorced his father. She claims that under the guise of the loving grandson he really came back for money and revenge (Miss Odelia distrusts banks and is rumored to have large sums of money hidden around the house). He appears to have gotten both before the sheriff carried him away for extradition to California. She said that before his final attack upon her he told his parole officer in a phone conversation she overheard that God was a black man and that he was God, and that revenge was his duty here on earth.

Miss Odelia was mauled and badly shaken, but not seriously injured. The sisters of the church rallied round with sympathetic visits and covered dishes; and she was, at least for a little while, no longer alone. But this event is only a respite in her growing alienation from the community. Always regarded as somewhat superior and "stand-offish" by virtue of her better education and independent ways, she has steadily withdrawn from church and social ties. The reasons may be many, but the sisters of the church say, "She shouldn't have moved off to build that big house," (only a block from

Jelly Roll), and that she has an obsessive fear of losing her money. Miss Odelia, on the other hand, makes several valid observations about the growing impersonality and cash-hungry disposition of the community, and she has suffered both real and threatened attempts to take away her savings.

The Reverend — living out the Word

CHAPTER 8

Deacon Clark

The Children of His Labor

James Clark, unlike so many of the retirees who line the streets of Jelly Roll, is sixty-seven, lean, alert, and still in his prime. Clear-eyed, thoughtful, and verbally skillful, self-educated with a broad knowledge of the Bible, he is a highly respected member of his community, a deacon in the large Willow Grove Baptist Church at the center of the black community. Son of a poor cotton farmer from south of Junction City, he moved to Calion in 1952 when another mill owned by the Company burned to the ground. At that time the Company moved its best employees to its expanding pallet manufacturing operations at Calion, and James, always a good worker, was among them. "When the mill at Junction burned, I left my people back at the homeplace and a town full of crooked white men; I crossed the bridge never turnin' back. I got no regrets."

James started work at Calion hand-nailing warehouse pallets, and when the plant was converted to the manufacture of furniture parts he eventually moved into the glue room in a semi-skilled position where he remained a conscientious employee with the kind of work record that would gladden any foreman's heart. Always seemingly content in his job, James is quick to point out that through most of these years opportunities for black advancement were mostly nonexistent. When the furniture plant was unionized in 1969 he quietly assumed a major role in its election drive. With the prestige of his church in the background, he gained the support of moderates in a close election. "I told 'em to let us negotiate with management for what we needed, not go beggin' to the office one by one." The union won a majority in the furniture plant, but lost in the other divisions. James, having keynoted its success, stepped aside to let others take credit and power; always a soft-spoken and philosophical man, he concluded the subject by remarking wryly, "and things don't change till they have to change."

James lives in one of the larger reconditioned old frame houses on Thomas Street directly across from the busy residence of Willie and Babe and just two doors from the home of Saphire Jones, "the night club," he calls it with a disgruntled nod of the head in that direction. Being a devout man who covets only peace and quiet he is perplexed by his fate of ending up engulfed by the sights and sounds of the "high life" he so disdains. At Saphire's there is "always drinkin', smokin' dope, young men and young mothers swayin' to the music, kissin' and floppin' around while their dirty children are lyin' on the floor like little pigs. Mothers, some still in school and some grey-headed, havin' a joint or shootin' dice on the floor." His face tightens as he speaks, there is emotion in his voice, he sits upright then slumps back in his chair. "They degrade themselves. It's the times. I can't keep up. Lucy Mobile is ninety-four, oldest member of our church, been livin' in the same yard for over sixty years! You think any of these young people gonna stay put six months? No, they got money, borrow it, or get it somehow, go where they please, when they please." James sat back, lost in a reverie from his own youth on the farm, the satisfaction of hard work, little money but plentiful good food, the vivid tastes and smells in youth remembered, all flattened by age, the slow passage of time and the seasons "when Christmas took as long to come as Leap Year does now."

Fittingly, James's house is surrounded by thick, head-high privet hedge with only a gap for his walk. He sits on his porch in hopeful meditation or preparing his Sunday School lessons, but flickering past the gap in the hedge is a steady stream of cars and pedestrians, and by 3:00 p.m. on a Friday afternoon the slamming of car doors and howling radios announce the arrival of the weekend party at Saphire's. In the middle of these distractions James struggles to concentrate and continue his recounting of the church's successful record, his voice rises to counteract the sounds from without, "Now we have a full-service Sunday School and youth department, and we have the Sunshine Boys who visit the sick and shut-ins. We need an education building and maybe we'll get it one of these days. Our pastor, Reverend Lambert, is a trustee in the

Arkansas Baptist College and President of the Columbus Association. The children put on Bible plays, a good way to learn to speak in public." I ask him about how many young couples attend.

> Only two or three regular, some just send their kids up the street. Mostly the older folks hold it all together; young don't have that old stickability. When they say, 'I'm ready, you can count on me,' then you know they won't be there! Oh, when there's troubles, things get drastic, they come to church; be the loudest singin' and the strongest prayer when somebody's hungry. Our biggest hang-up these days is too much prosperity. We're too weak to endure it. When there's a big funeral we'll have 'em packed to the door — see who's gonna cry, how they're put away.

Although James is acutely conscious of his church's moral leadership in the black community, he is equally disdainful of those "out in the woods evangelical churches," such as the one led by a neighbor that relies heavily on emotion and little on teaching and moral example. "Now that Holy Hill Church is just a few folks livin' the sawmill life. They had a good revival lately, say there was some pretty good fallin' out and they poured a lotta oil; but the preachin' got too strong and run some folks off."

The din from the neighbors and the street grows louder. The porch where we sit alone is like the calm eye of a hurricane winding up all around us. As I strain to hear his soft voice he continues his thoughts. "History repeats itself. The Bible tells us about times like these, too much of what we don't need, not enough of what we do. We've broken the laws of God and nature and man before, but God will have the last word." I tried to ask him about his long marriage and many children. He is reluctant to answer, shakes his head and continues, "Let's not talk on that now, I don't try to count 'em up, some good, some bad, most are knockin' on nothin' but my door is always open." And indeed it is, for the home of this elderly couple is crawling with small grandchildren whom James attempts to ignore.

After talking a bit longer in generalities, he returns reluctantly to the subject of his children.

> We allowed our children to get away with everything. We bore the pain for our children, we bonded them out of jail. We let them be dependent. We spoiled them with all the things we never had. They thanked us with extravagance, resentment. We let them get too close, didn't keep enough space between the generations, and as you see next door some parents are even keeping company with their children in their vices! They get softer each generation, and this country of ours is going down.

Such attitudes are part of a Biblical way of speaking and thinking as well as an aura of quiet sadness that surrounds James Clark despite an outwardly courtly air and good humor. His wife, Riva, says he worries about all the problems in the newspaper, things we cannot change. In their forty years of marriage she has borne and raised eleven children. In her own catalogue of names, places and jobs they hold she reports proudly and first that one is in the Army Air Force in Japan, a daughter is a nurse in an El Dorado hospital, two girls are off "somewhere in Detroit," another works at the local poultry plant. She speaks sadly, remotely of the first-born, James, Jr., away somewhere; and then there is "live-at-home Bob," an alcoholic who works sporadically in Calion. With so many potentially productive lives raised in such a proper, God-fearing, work-oriented household, one can't help but ask the question, what went wrong with so many of their children? Riva's only remark is that "we take things as they come." Does this family dramatize the toll to be paid by blacks for poor schools and job prejudice? James's summary of his brood's few successes and many failures does not dwell upon social injustice. "They got breaks I never dreamed of, but some of them are just knockin' on nothin', buried up somewhere in raggedy apartments! James — Shirley — Helen — Bob, all knockin' on nothin'. Don't know where they are, and don't give a damn. Bring home nothin' but their troubles, but my door is always open."

While academicians may dwell upon the effects of environment and the social system, this black community, on the whole, does not. The preponderant view of old and young alike is neither despair nor self pity, only resentful sometimes that whites have made their burden heavier or strewn the path to success with clever traps, but that ultimately each man's success or failure is determined by his own inner strength or weakness. Parents blame not themselves nor society but their children for their own failures. Lacking more typically middle-class shame and self recrimination, they believe their children's destiny to be largely in their own hands.

James and Riva Clark have been directly affected by their own children's family problems. Their old house is crowded with six grandchildren that have been "left on the doorstep" by their various children caught in financial and domestic crises. James retired over a year ago, but pressing financial needs sent him back to the furniture plant to work out his maximum retirement income before the heat of summer. Recently, however, he began to experience dizzy spells and had to return home with a diagnosis of low blood pressure and ulcers. He is now trapped by the burden of raising a second family and too old to set things straight. "The church folks say to me, 'James, you done had and still got more kids than anybody in Calion'." To add to the worries of supporting six grandchildren, their own children use them as a "crash pad" periodically, and their second-youngest son Bob, "a part-time worker and full-time alcoholic," contributing only erratic support, still lives with them.

The subject of eleven children and his present dilemma makes James squirm with discomfort.

> If I had it to do over again, I'd have just two kids, but I was one of nine myself! And back on the farm everybody made hisself useful. Riva and I had just two before I went into service in 1941; but after I came out in '45 seems like she had one every time I turned around! She never complained or had no troubles till after the last one when the doctor told her about some medicine to keep from havin' 'em. I asked her why she didn't get that medicine twenty years before! Of course, doctors never told me nothin', either. I wouldn't buy nothin' — always seemed too late when I thought of it. Anyway, without all these children I might not still be with this woman of mine. As it was I never went anywhere. Sometimes some of the boys would holler at me, 'Clark, can't you ever get out?' Sure, I could have done what I pleased, but I didn't want to run around, couldn't afford it, no how.

His house is always neat, clean, and well maintained, with roses blooming at the doorstep. However, the simplicity of their life styles, the absence of the ubiquitous automobile in the driveway, no pile of bikes, wagons, skates or other expensive toys for their children, and the plainness of their furnishings make it obvious that all their income and labor have been devoted to bringing up two generations.

On the surface everything seemed the same at the time of my last interview: Riva still quietly, unobtrusively goes about the business of cooking, washing, and caring for her children and grandchildren alike. Except for the unrelenting blare of the television set in the living room, there is a quiet order here even when all six children are milling about. No boisterous arguments or shrill demands, neither screams of laughter not pain, for these children are being raised under the strict constraints common to an older generation. Still, beyond the surface calm, the smell of pot roast on the stove, the neat privet hedge, and the obedient children, a man sits alone, strained to the limits of his tolerance and wondering out loud, "Why me!"

Heretofore, always too proud and independent to ask for welfare, his present financial burden and ill health have left him little choice. James Clark, in what should be his easy years of retirement, has been compelled to assume what he perceives to be the indignities and shame associated with a welfare household. His circumstances are often repeated in Calion when aging parents agree to keep grandchildren brought to them under diverse situations or distress, or simply in denial of responsibility. But when grandparents consent to take these grandchildren in, they can count on the support of the welfare system. The Social Security Act provides financial assistance to eligible grandparents with legally adopted grandchildren; or abandoned children can receive aid under AFDC without reference to grandparents' income. In addition, the grandparents are entitled to food stamps and Medicaid coverge with certain income qualifications. While providing a more humane alternative for unwanted or unaffordable children, this can also be a path of least resistance for their biological parents, as well as an unwanted burden placed upon grandparents such as the Clarks.

PART II

The Middle Aged and Traditional Families

Transition, Conflict, and Accommodation Between Old and New

CHAPTER 9

Ruby Johnson

A Single Mother and Her Clan

Welfare mothers are often depicted as helpless victims of their own fertility, caught in an environment of poverty and uncontrollable circumstances. In the bloom of youth, the "welfare mother" probably had the support of several men, but the pregnancies that followed made her less appealing, often over-weight, and ultimately, left alone with the offspring of her various romances. Early or late, she falls back upon the support system of the state, encumbered by child care, often uneducated, and without employable skills. As such she has been branded a public liability about whom much has been written, and for whom even more has been prescribed. This stereotype is particularly applicable to women of middle age.

Older welfare mothers in Jelly Roll often characterize themselves as victims of male fickleness and their own ignorance, their fate sealed before they scarcely knew what had happened. Ruby Johnson is a fitting example. Now a heavy-set forty-two, she was one of six children born to poor but hard-working parents. She got "knocked up" at fifteen and has since had eight children by a succession of men while she lived most of the time in her parent's large frame house on Mill Street. The youngest is now eight and, as Ruby puts it,

> We were stupid girls, kept completely ignorant. My

own Mama told me that if a boy touched me, I'd have a baby. And I still hate to be touched! [Laughs] So don't you or nobody else ever touch me, hear? Why even when I got married I didn't know nothin'. We came from the wedding to this very house, and when he started getting all over me, I got right out of that bed and went and got in bed with my Mama. She should have told me the score, but always just said I'd have to learn it from experience same as she did. . . . Yeah, we were stupid and we stayed that way, even after the babies started comin' every year. Used to be every time I got pregnant I'd ask the doctor what to do, and he'd lay some crap on be 'bout keepin' my legs crossed or my skirt from over my head. I tried to get those men to use somethin', but you know how men are!

Although a long-term welfare recipient who currently receives $552 per month in welfare and food stamps, Ruby has little good to say about the system that sustains her:

Sure it helps, but I wish I had a good payin' job. I make every one of my children work, first at home and then outside, because welfare ain't gonna save you. . . . When the babies come the men are gonna leave. I never asked for one single baby. If I'd known what these kids of mine know today none of them would be here! And I'd have me some fancy job uptown. Men are so selfish. They're takers — fast talk and fast walk. So why do these girls get pregnant now? They know better, but have a baby to try an' keep their man. Won't work. Drives 'em away. But what do they know? Nothin'! Never even learned to wash dishes. All they ever done is loaf on the streets, listen to the disco beat. How ya gonna make a family outta that?

Calion is a full-employment community because the mill and furniture plant give preference on all hiring to local labor. Nonetheless, welfare is a pervasive force and source of income here. Many black households receive some form of social service income. Elderly retired couples such as the Clarks and Coles receive Supplemental Social Security benefits for grandchildren whom they have adopted when parents defaulted on their responsiblities. Also, a number of young mothers live with their parents while receiving Aid to Families with Dependent Children. In some cases, young mothers have formed separate households and illegally receive payments when the natural father or another man is living with them and providing some income. In still other instances, older women, like Ruby Johnson, live in households legally without men or known external sources of income, choosing the security of the welfare system and its deceptive ease rather than venturing out into the labor market. As the following welfare arithmetic demonstrates, this is not an irrational decision:

Ruby's Welfare Income:

$320.00 Monthly Total Social Service Income
232.00 Monthly Food Stamps
$552.00 Monthly plus Medicaid

Ruby's Alternative:
Entry Level Unskilled Job at Mill:

$827.00 Monthly
60.84 (less) Federal & State Income Tax
$766.16
55.41 (less) FICA
$710.75
31.00 (less) 80% coverage Medical
$695.75 Net take-home pay

On the face of it, Ruby has made a prudent choice not to work for the narrow spread between welfare income and net wages, a spread that melts to nothing when transportation, baby sitter, and clothing costs become a factor. The simple truth of the matter is that most welfare recipients "net out" at an amount approximating prevailing entry level unskilled jobs, an amount designed to meet the bare essentials of a living wage. Only if welfare is supplemented by a working or "hustling" man illegally around the house can it provide a comfortable life style. Therefore, the decision not to seek work is often neither slothful nor unwise, but rather the best temporary coping strategy that ignores any possible advancement through acquired skills that could lead to better wages.

Ruby is the first to attest that, for those who play it straight, welfare benefits keep you "just one step ahead of the wolf." There are no amenities. First priority upon Ruby's social service cash income of $320.00 per month are the following typical bills:

Arkansas Power & Light Co. (averaging) (heating & one window air conditioner)	$156.00
Arkla Gas Company (gas grate, stove, water heater)	37.00
City of Calion (water and sewer)	42.00
Supplies (non-food stamp items)	55.00
TOTAL	$290.00

This leaves a scant $30.00 per month to cover clothing and contingencies for herself and five children living at home. Although Ruby lives with her mother in her mother's house which is fully paid for, she is expected to help with maintenance, repairs, and appliance breakdowns.

Obviously, these figures do not work out. There is just not enough to cover the many essentials and contingencies for this large family. When Ruby and I first talked about the budgetary discrepancy she inferred that there were other occasional sources of income to meet emergencies, all of which she vaguely referred to as her "hustles." In the midst of my general puzzlement over how this family could possibly make ends meet, I was taken aback one afternoon by the discovery that Ruby had recently acquired a handsome, late model Pontiac which she showed off with beaming good humor. The title to the car was in her name as was the obligation to pay twelve more monthly notes for $164.00 each. The $1,600.00 down payment had been made by a "gentleman friend," and Ruby exuberantly added, "Man, have I got a good deal goin' now!"

After my initial surprise I realized that I had made the same error so often made by those that study or administer to women of fatherless households, namely, the false assumption that they live alone in some sort of social and economic vacuum. The fact of the matter is that their unorthodox associations with men have long confounded the statisticians and the administrators of welfare to the point where, as a matter of operational necessity, most welfare mothers have to be considered as independent family units. Nothing could be further from the truth. In reality, both socially and psychologically, it is naive to assume that women, either in youth or in middle age, would often live without consorts. And, in communities where sex is regarded as a merchantable commodity, the liasons of most welfare mothers can command financial rewards. Ruby Johnson illustrated this perfectly. Seen alone, her finances cannot support her family's present life style. The "hustle" is the missing variable.

Ruby, over several years, had cultivated a casual affair with an older man until it had grown into a close, meaningful relationship. Recently, he had made the large down payment on her car so that, "I could come to him when I pleased, and without the whole world knowing my business." He had also given her several credit cards to use whenever her children needed shoes or clothing, a major contribution to the family budget. Then, unfortunately and without warning, "her man" had a serious and debilitating stroke:

> He was a nice man. He made things easy for me, but his kids never liked me. When he had to move in with them, because of his health, they shut me out. I never go there any more. All we can do is talk on the telephone. The other day, he asked me, 'Have you found you another good man to take

care of you?' Well, what could I say? Who's gonna find another man to fill those size thirteen shoes? Anyhow, these young girls have ruined the market. They don't give a damn; they'll go down for a six pack. They don't know how to build up a relationship. Now it's tougher than hell for me. I hate to lose that nice car with only eight notes left for it to be mine. But how am I gonna make a $164.00 monthly payment? How am I gonna keep clothes on these kids? I gotta break loose and make me a new hustle. But it's tough! The competition is out there, and it's not easy for me. Too many men, too many babies, and each baby you have takes a little more passion out of you. By the time you reach my age [42], it takes a lot of patting and rubbing to get me interested. I'm really tired of it all.

So, for many, welfare is the foundation but not the superstructure of their family economics. Because these amorous matches are so frequently tenuous and transient, they provide only a variable and insecure source of income that must be quickly replaced when lost. Herein lies the most unstable component of the matriarchal household; for without the hustle or some other secondary lifeline of support the welfare mother is, as advertised, living on the ragged edge of poverty.

In those precarious circumstances it is understandable why money matters dominate the conversation. Faced with a chronic shortage of ready cash, Ruby looks back longingly at her youth and better times:

> These kids of mine got no work and can't find any. Growing up with idle hands. When we were kids, Mr. Tom Goodwin always had plenty of cotton to chop. Now here's the County Fair rollin' round again and I got no money for 'em! Mama, you watch her, will give my kids her money for medicine so they can go. Their hands are always out for somethin' — school supplies, raffles, a present for the teacher, go somewhere, eat somethin', buy this, buy that. I never had to ask for money. If I wanted something I could damn well work to get it, but these idle children got nothin' but time to think on what they haven't got. . . . and how can I teach them sharing and concern for others in these selfish times? When my own daughter will dump her children on me while she goes to the lake. They'll eat here, but does she offer me a bag of groceries or a five-dollar bill? Hell, no! It's take, take, take. The responsibility for all these kids and all the neighbors' is all mine. I can't even keep ice water in the refrigerator. They're all over this place with their loud voices, talking big an' showin' out. Know nothin', learnin' nothin', talkin' all the time. They don't have to mind at

home so why mind me. Without discipline this place would be a mad house. Who remembers when little girls had to be seen but silent?

Christmas is a particularly traumatic time for the welfare family. The television set repetitively hawks the splendors of middle class consumption. The message is received at every level in the family, and as the day approaches there are growing expectations side by side with strident disclaimers from mother that anything is forthcoming. For the head of the household, it is a time of growing anxiety, a time to profess bankruptcy while making frantic loans, calling in old obligations, scrounging all the cash you can so that everyone can have Christmas.

Despite the main purchases of practical presents, new shoes and jeans, sweaters and shirts, there is mounting pressure to blow precious resources on at least one high-priced electronic game of Atari, PacMan, or Donkey Kong. And just when you think you have scraped it all together, a last-minute call comes for help from relatives. In Ruby's household this year, it was her second-oldest daughter, Alice Jean, laid off at the hospital just before Christmas, with four young sons "like stair steps and no husband," who implored her mother for just a hundred dollars to buy new shoes for her boys:

> Now, Alice Jean don't ask for nothin' less she really needs it. There she was sittin' crying on the telephone with nothin' laid by for Christmas. Husband? she got nothin' but one of those Sonny Boys living with her that feed off you and contribute nothin' but stud service. So there I was tryin' to hustle my own kids, who are working, for twenty bucks apiece so that Alice Jean could get something together. But their checks are all spoken for before they get them. They make their commitments too far out, and then they're in your face, too, asking for money when you need help from them. So here I go, back to Crab Apple [local loan shark]. Seems I'm cursed to see after this family forever!

Under the pressure to come through for this house full of children of all ages at Christmas Ruby and her mother put the heat on their kinship network. Ruby called all of her brothers from Los Angeles to Kalamazoo, "Hi,honey, Mama wants to talk to you" was her usual line; and after the introductory amenities there was always a solicitation of hard cash. No stone was left unturned. Married children, working anthropologists were all touched for a loan or contribution to the greater glory of the Yuletide season.

Ruby's children have not missed the lessons of their mother's domestic entrapment. As we shall see, each of her children has modified his or her behavior with varying degrees of success to avoid a similar fate. Indeed, going from door to door in Jelly Roll, one finds fewer children delivered by each succeeding generation; for "livin' the sawmill life with eight or ten kids runnin' around" has definitely fallen from favor. This does not mean that the welfare option goes unexercised — having a first baby in the teens, becoming a little mother, possibly escaping from an unhappy home life, still holds its appeal. Like her mother and grandmother before her, biological maternity remains a powerful magnet, a way of life made easier by welfare.

Ruby Johnson now lives with her elderly mother in the largest old frame house on Mill Street. The original house was built in 1916 by her grandfather, Rufus Johnson, who had come to Calion to help build the first mill. Rufus was a strong family man and a respected community leader among blacks and whites alike. He became something of a local patriarch, lived to age ninety-seven and saw five generations in the house he built. He died in 1975 and was survived by his third wife, Anna, her six children, and some thirty grandchildren. Their old country house, though modified through the years, still had a recognizable long center hall extending from the front porch, with rooms opening on to it from either side, to a rear kitchen and pantry that extended across the entire back of the house. The view from the front door was down the long hall into the kitchen, and upon my first visit to the house on a hot summer's afternoon, a dozen small children were peeping out from every room to see who was at the door. I was ushered into the living room, or TV room as it is now called, by an older teenage girl carrying in one hand a switch at least five feet long. I was introduced to Ruby's mother, Mrs. Anna Johnson, who was seated in a stately manner on the sofa with the best view of the television set. As the conversation quickly turned to the old days, small children began to return to the television room; silently they filed in and took their places upon the floor like latecomers to the theater. Unlike the bedlam that reigned in many houses I have visited, there was an enforced quiet here, save for the steady drone of the television. If several children began to scuffle or argue, the long switch instantly flicked out over the tops of their heads, and the children would pull back silently in unquestioned obedience. Old Mrs. Johnson began a long reminiscence of her younger days in Calion: the ladies of the church sitting out under a spreading oak tree on a sticky summer's day to do their quilting and needle work, maybe engage in a spelling bee to teach each other a little reading. She looked back on a more trusting, open and cooperative spirit in those days, especially among the women of the town, and a uniform standard of conduct that is no more. She thought nothing, then, of disciplining her neighbors' children exactly like her own, something that today could cause quite a scene. She spoke nostalgically about the town's open spaces in the past when, "round about and behind everybody had a big vegetable garden, chickens and pigs, where you could see smartly in every direction as far as the highway and the railroad tracks." That the mill workers then were nearly all backyard farmers is a point often raised by old timers when comparing present and past wages. They emphasize that far less money was needed in times past in what was, in essence, a mixed barter and cash economy. Mrs. Johnson laments also the loss of social exchanges that accompanied the barter economy in which labor, goods, services, and social allegiances were intermingled:

> Money wasn't needed 'cept for salt and flour; bought no ice, kept milk for the babies and butter to cool in the well. Why even the doctor was lucky to get two dollars or a jar of peaches. And nobody went hungry either. Folks felt put here to help other Christians. Everybody did his share and got his share in return.

The conversion of the local community to an all-cash economy was a function of prosperity. It radically modified social relationships, attitudes, and life styles which culminated in Anna Johnson's recollection of her husband's last years. "Rufus was down for thirteen years 'fo he died. You know, only five people, 'cept family, came to see him in all that time. Turned out for the funeral, but where had they been?

No wonder, then, that the older generation feels such a bitter loss in the present. Symptomatically they seem to dwell disdainfully upon the cooking and eating habits of the younger generation many of whom, they claim, "ain't never seen nothin' to eat that didn't come with a wrapper on it." Nor is there rejoicing among older workers for present relatively high wage scales, even when compared with the "dollar a day 1930s;" while much praise is reserved for the machines that have mechanized the lumber handling industry and eliminated most of the back-breaking jobs that sawmilling once entailed.

Although some old timers and even a few middle-aged men still have gardens out back, gardening is becoming a lost art. Consequently, much open land around individual houses and around the town has grown up in tall weeds and is reverting to pine forest for lack of a willing plow. With the decline in gardening go also the skills in preserving and canning, even the proper preparation of fruits and vegetables that are in turn dropped from the diet in favor of processed foods. The Johnson's pantry brings back memories of the country store with shelves filled with jars of pickled cabbage and okra, peas, beans, preserved peaches, plum and pears. But the younger generation lacks the will and rejects the model of mother and grandmother who excel in the domestic crafts of food preparation, preservation, needle craft or other related skills. There are no home-canning heroines on television these days (unlike the old radio "soaps" which had their Ma Perkins, Molly Goldberg and Houseboat Hannah). Now modern roles models are the sleek ladies who concentrate on face, hair and the body beautiful while they pursue exciting careers. So the young mother identifies with the opposite of what she has seen at home, not the remembered smells of soap powders and cooking oils, but rather some eau de cologne.

Despite considerable drain upon the budget, even the non-working young mother does a minimum of cooking. If she is a home with one or more small children, she follows a predictable routine of visiting, child care and TV watching that is only briefly interrupted by housekeeping and food preparation.

The Johnsons keep open house for all comers every day of the year. There are Ruby's six brothers and their families, her own adult daughters and their seven children, five adopted children, plus friends, and neighbors who come and go with regularity, some to visit all day or just an hour. For visiting here is traditionally intense, frequent and economic. Old Mrs. Johnson measures her closeness and affection for her children by how often they come to visit. Daughters may leave their children every day to be cared for while they are at work, a heavy imposition accepted without complaint or reimbursement. As Mrs. Johnson puts it, "I don't put a price on it, sometimes they'll surprise me with a little somethin' and make me feel good." Rather, the rewards for baby sitting are apparent in the warmth and solicitude bestowed upon the sitters. There is usually a lingering visit both upon infant delivery and retrieval — nothing equivalent to the surburban syndrome of dumping children hastily on grandmother while parents, in a rush, slam car doors as they depart for the movies.

Children are everywhere, but the Johnsons somehow run a well-ordered household. There are many little indications that there is "no man around the house;" screens are pushed out and the house swarms with flies, the back door hangs loose upon its hinges so that chickens periodically slip in to roam the corridors, door knobs malfunction if present at all. But things that respond well to kid power or show the traditional woman's touch, like the kitchen and dining room, are well scrubbed and orderly. Children sweep the floors several times a day.

As any day progresses, a switch, the symbol of authority, passes from grandmother to mother to an older daughter and back again as the role of protector, treasurer, nurse and psychiatrist is silently shared by the senior adults. Ruby plays the part flamboyantly in counterpoint to her mother's stern reserve. The presence of so many children serves to attract more; since the Johnson children are kept close to home under constant supervision, the neighborhood naturally gravitates toward them. With a tolerant smile Ruby remarks, "Well, we got the neighborhood here on the floor [watching TV]. If I run 'em out the front door they come right in the back. A house full don't bother me, but teens! That's somethin' else.

The household radiates protective concern, but without touching or demonstrative affection. If a child comes in hurt or mistreated there is a sympathetic binding up of wounds or redress of grievances, but the balm of affectionate caresses is missing; or rather it is reserved almost exclusively for the very small children who are pampered, cuddled and lapped much of the time. Young mothers and older children with time on their hands occupy themselves with the grooming and dressing of infants and small children almost like playing at dolls. This play aspect is apparent in the popularity of such elaborate and time-consuming hair styles as pig tails and corn rowing. Small children are accustomed to sitting for hours on mothers' or surrogates' laps where an entire nap of an hour or more may be enjoyed. Small children are seldom allowed to roam far or at will; a single step from porch to yard is regarded as a precipice, a toy horse, a dangerous mount. They are encouraged to stay close and come back to open arms for solace in all adversities.

The sudden end to this tactile phase by no later than age three brings on a total about-face in which affectionate contact becomes taboo. Instead, strict disciplinary demands and physical punishment are the rule. Ruby appears among her quarreling children with the threat, 'I'm comin' out to whip the captain and the whole crew." Sometimes she does just that, although the threat will usually suffice. This two-step phasing of child rearing may well have its origins in the traditionally large families where the infant was weaned by age two or sooner to make way for a new baby, thereby forcing a decisive separation of the mother and her previous child. There is also an implied sexual basis for non-contact after two or three, since the prevailing wisdom suggests either personal embarrassment and concern on the part of adults that any fondling, even of the very young, will be sexually stimulating. With so many people, young and old, living in close quarters without much privacy, a hands-off policy rigidly reinforces the sexual repression of the young and may explain the exuberant release subsequently in the teens, when all forms of physical contact connote sexual intent.

Ruby and her mother have an all-encompassing child rearing philosophy that is expounded and applied with equal vigor:

I've never had any trouble with my kids. I'm just the same with all of them. If they don't mind us they won't mind others out yonder. I start spankin' while they're still in diapers. Discipline makes everybody happy. And everybody gets a job to do, around the house at first, then outside raking the yard, feedin' the chickens, housekeepin' till they get big enough to work at odd jobs around the neighborhood and earn a few dollars. What good they gonna be if I have to wake them up, wash their face and put their pants on for 'em. All of them know what to do cuz they do like I do. Same way at school. No problem. I tell their teachers to whip 'em, lay that paddle on them, don't send 'em home. They're in school to learn. I got no dropouts. They all make good grades. Teachers speak well of them, and I never had a single child sent home.

This tight parental discipline has produced neither sullen nor resentful children. On the contrary, I have seldom seen such an exuberant self-possessed tribe. As Ruby puts it with more pride than annoyance,

Now it's a struggle to keep anything to eat or drink in this house. Food just disappears. Give 'em a dollar or a nickel and they're at the cafe buyin' something. I try to keep the corn crib full, but these kids are real educated. Now don't set down a six pack of beer or cokes and walk off. When you come back, it'll look just like you left it, but every can will be empty. How do they get those tabs back in flat? Amazin' kids!

Their sleeping arrangements also reflect a disciplined household as well as the realities of their community. Ruby has a small bedroom to herself where her mother also naps, "to keep from goin' crazy sometimes," but her mother regularly sleeps in the large bedroom where she presides over a dormitory for all the girls, while the boys sleep scattered around the house. Ruby comments,

We never know who's comin' through this house. You'd be surprised how many neighbors leave their kids here till all hours of the night. They got all the time to get these babies, but no time to fool with them. Let the street raise 'em! Don't miss 'em even after ten at night. They're raisin' 'em for the penitentiary, that's what.

Voices of the Children

Sally, age twenty-eight, is Ruby's oldest child:

I was raised up in this same old house of Granny's with eleven other kids, six of us and six of my uncle's. It sounds wild but it wasn't. Everything went pretty smooth most of the time. Grandmother's policy was to get everybody up early, hit the floor at 5:00 a.m. We bathed, cleaned up the house, did our laundry and everything before we went to school. Sometimes when I was just too sleepy to get up, I'd get out of my bed and slip into another. But you couldn't put it past Granny. You'd get a glass of cold water down your neck and that would make your mind up. Granny and my grandfather were very strict, put the belt on us for steppin' out of line. Mother was too, but my grandparents ran the show. My father didn't live with us long. He still lives here in Calion, but I don't see him much. Sometimes we talk on the street. Really, my grandfather was my daddy. A boyfriend never came through the door without his permission. They didn't let me date until I was almost seventeen; so right off I fell in love and you know how it is with that first love. Well, I was a very ignorant school girl. Nobody told you nothin' when I was growing up. I got pregnant in a hurry. It was my senior year in high school, and I was crazy to play on the basketball team. Good, too. But I had to give it up. Really broke by heart. I had so wanted to play on the team, but there I was getting big with that baby in me. My grandparents insisted we get married. No bastards for our family. I had a beautiful daughter, but being married at eighteen had cut off all my pleasures. I'd lost out with the team, and before long, I was back home without a husband. Now, I've started early and worked hard with my girls (ages eight and ten). I tell them all about the birds and bees and how gettin' pregnant will ruin your life.

Around here lotsa mothers act like they're glad to be grandmothers when their little girls get pregnant. Everybody talks proud and nobody mentions an abortion. So what have you got? Babies takin' care of babies.! Not me. I want the best for my kids, good jobs, careers.

I got pregnant again the year after Sally was born. Nice boy from Norphlet [small nearby town]. We were so in love! He was in the Army, and I became an Army wife, moving around the country. I sure enjoyed it. This little girl from Calion hadn't seen much before. I especially liked livin' in Texas and going to Laredo in Old Mexico to shop and eat. After a few years my husband got a full medical disability and we moved back to Norphlet, right near his folks. Now I've got him a baby boy. He's got his son, so no more babies. I'm stayin' on those little pills till I grow old. Now I'm fishin', but not every day. (Sally has since taken a job at the mill.)

Allen, age fourteen:

I'm second oldest in this house, really, cuz all my older sisters are married or moved out, and my oldest brother, Robert, sort of comes and goes. I like it when he's here. Yes, he's like a Dad to me. He's the only one I got. [Do you miss not having a father at home?] Can't say's I do. When you got two older brothers, do you need one? Some of the kids I know got dads that are tough. I get along with my brothers, Mama and Grandma. Barry [his older brother, age seventeen] is a running back on the first-string football team. Really good. Sometimes he shows me how to throw a block and stuff like that. . . ." [How are you doing in school?] My lowest grade is 81. That's in math. It's funny cuz that's my favorite subject except for P.E. My grades are all good, and I like school OK. You better not bring home any bad grade or POW!

Barry's goin' into the Army soon as he graduates. So am I. I like new experiences. It's hard to tell in the position I'm in, later I might change my mind, but after I'm in the Army for maybe four years, I'll come back and be a roving construction worker — good money and a good job. Then, maybe, I'll be a policeman like on TV [laughs]. No matter what they dream about most of the boys end up at the mill. Not me.

I got to go to New Orleans this spring with the Baseball All Stars. That's my best game. We had a big barbecue, got to go fishin' and swimmin'. [Did you get to tour the city?] We drove thru lot'sa city on the bus till we got to a nice camping place. Everybody had a real good time. Last year I had a chance to visit my uncle in California, but I turned it down. It's so boring in the city — just sit around and watch TV. When I'm at home, I'm out the door. Always somethin' goin' on on this street. . . . I like to travel on the bus with the team or on school trips. I've been as far as Little Rock. With the team you get to go everywhere and are never bored. Barry says if you're really good you can play college football. I'd like to do that without going to college [laughs]. There's no place like home. . . . Sometimes my sisters make me mad, when they tell on you for doing something you didn't really do — then, I'm out the door! I'm the first one up every morning when school is on. I get the paper, take a bath before the rush, do my homework and it's time to go. . . . All my dreams are in front of me. What will I dream tonight? What will happen tomorrow? Will I be a star and put those dudes down on the football field?

Suzie, age ten, is short and rather plump with a frequent radiant smile:

I like most everything — all my teachers and all my friends. I never sit in the back of the school bus. That's where they get into trouble. I sit up front behind the driver. It's never noisy there, and I'm the quietest one on the bus.

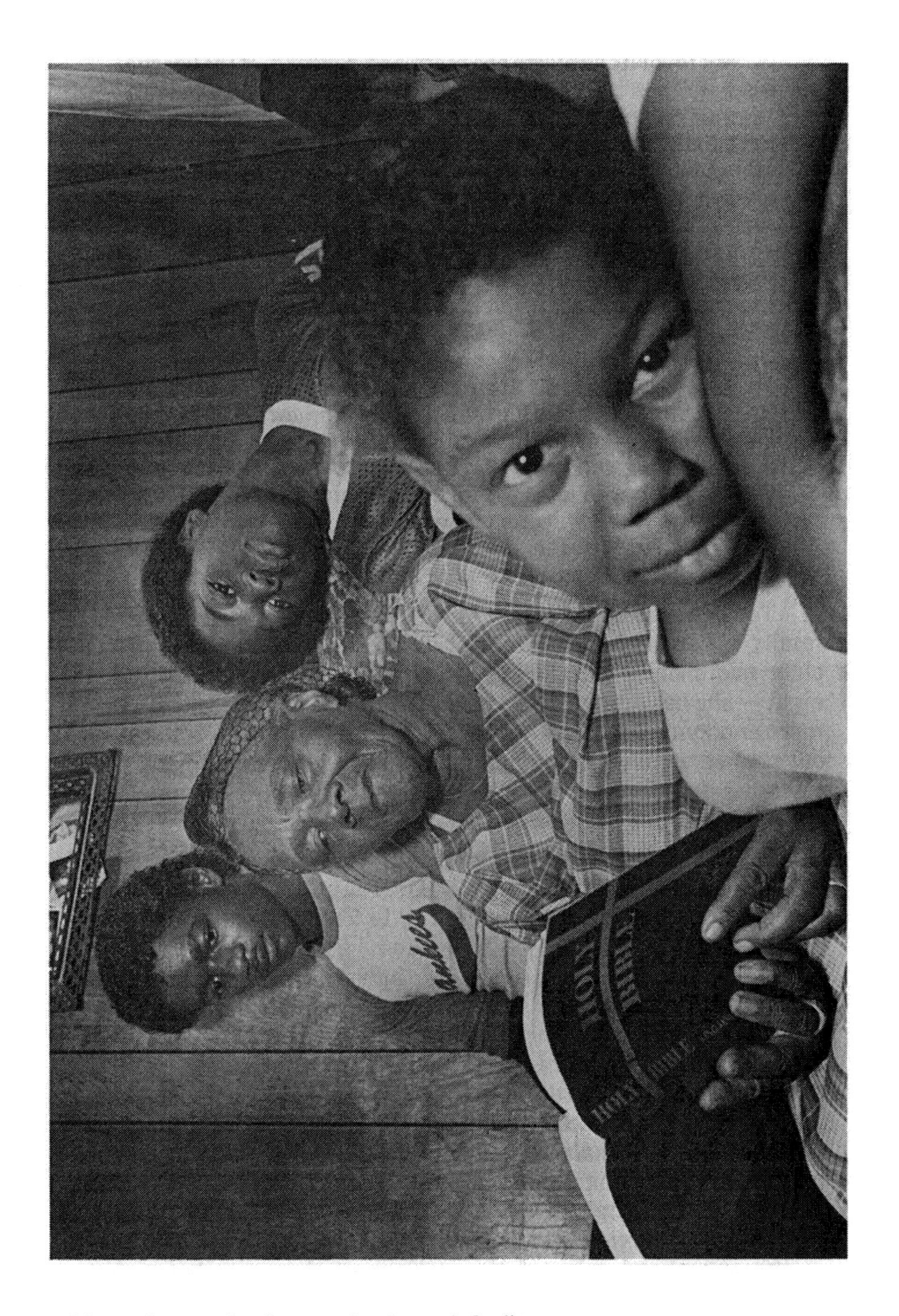

"Grandma raised us strict but right."

. . . My favorite subjects are math and reading. It makes me mad if I don't always make good grades. . . . I get awful tired of cleaning up the house every day. The girls alway have to do it, and the boys mess it up the most. Sandra, Pris and me are always the ones that work. Mama or Grandma always call us to clean up the mess. Sandra likes to take care of the babies. She always wins at that . Carry 'em around so's they don't cry and get everybody upset. I'd sooner play baseball out back when the boys don't play too rough; then I quit or call Grandma. Sometimes Allen makes me mad. He's rough. He teases. Then I go to Grandma and watch TV or help Sandra with the baby. . . . My favorite programs are first: 'Chips'; second: 'Give Me a Break'; and third: 'Different Strokes.' Homework is easy so I watch TV every night until 10:00. We all get up at 5:00 every day for school. . . . [What do yo wish for the most?] Enough money to go to the fair. It's comin' soon. Mama gets real upset when she don't have enough money to take us. When I grow up I'm gonna make lot'sa money being a policewoman. Then I'll be able to do whatever I want.

Today Ruby is still very involved with this large extended family in her mother's house. But as her own children have grown older and shouldered more responsibility — her youngest is now eight — she has drifted away from "that house full of little troubles" more and more. She likes to take off on all-day fishing trips or hang out at a beer joint while her mother and Ruby's older daughters "run the home front" and a whole new generation of infants and small children that has been passed down to them.

To make matters worse, Ruby is still "between men." Her "hustle" has lost much of its old appeal. "Mr. Right" has failed to make a timely appearance. She is struggling to keep her car from being repossessed, her "four wheels to freedom" from the teeming household, its unrelenting absence of privacy and unquenchable demands. She has grown increasingly short with her family and become obsessed with the probable loss of her car. She makes regular trips to town, frequently visits the welfare office making new demands, despite recent cutbacks in her allowances; and haggles with the gas company and meter readers as the bills mount on all sides. She talks half-heartedly of getting a job, but with a partially immobilized hand hurt in an automobile accident years ago, her lack of skills and the recession, there are few prospects other than domestic service, which she shuns. Ruby feels totally trapped — the subsidized roles of the welfare mother now leaves her stranded. She looks for escape, but her past decisions bear unmercifully upon her future options:

Life's been tough for me; sometimes I've begged for our next meal. I know all the whites in Calion because I've worked for most of them one time or another. Don't you know it's hard facin' all those people down — me and all those babies and no husband in sight. Chasing their daddies down on pay day tryin' to beg a few dollars for the babies they'd made.

All these kids! I didn't ask for nair one of them. Prayed I wouldn't have 'em, but they kept comin'. You know, I married young, only once, to the only man that didn't get me pregnant [laughs]. That's real funny, ain't it? But the others, they kept punchin' holes in my life. . . . I was young then, so in love and all that bullshit, excuse me, I'd be housekeepin' with my man and out whoring to make enough money to keep him happy and the babies fed. . . . then getting knocked up again, fallin' out with one man, turnin' round and fallin' in with another. All those years I kept Mama in a state of shock, but, bless her, she kept this old house goin', nursed Papa and helped take care of my babies. I finally had to slow down [laughs].Quit off havin' babies. Phew! Praise the Lord! We was gettin' 'em raised somehow without their daddies and gettin' 'em out of the nest. But Mama, she had gotten so used to taking mine in, I guess she couldn't break the habit, so she started takin' in kinfolks' children: Brian and Beverly and Albert and Melinda. So now here we are all rolled up in this shack full of kids — and the babies keep comin'. I'm sick of it, I'll tell you. They bring their love to Granny, but the bill collectors come lookin' for me. Mama sits back and says, 'The Lord will provide.' But I'm the one out scrapping and scratchin' to pay the electric. . . .

I've had a life, haven't I? I can still laugh about it, but it don't come so easy any more. The only peace I get is when I go to the lake — sit there all day, sometimes. I don't care if I got a worm on my hook [laughs]. My nerves are shot. Believe me! I gotta get a place of my own, a little peace and quiet, a little privacy, a chance to entertain a gentleman friend, have me a man.

You see, you've got to help me get a house of my own. Most of my kids have let me down. They've got jobs and good money, but none of it stays here — sometimes they'll give me or Mama a ten-dollar bill. What's ten dollars gonna buy these days? Ellen has moved out, Sally's mad, and I'm giving Albert his walkin' papers because he won't pay for nothin'. Who needs them!

If I had a place separate from Mama, just me and my three youngest kids, I would be able to get a nice housing allowance to pay the rent and work part-time without mes-

> sin' up my welfare. I'm not kiddin', it'll work. I've been to the welfare office, and they laid it all out for me — livin' with Mama and her check keeps me from getting a good check of my own. Crazy isn't it? What I need is a good rent house to rent in Calion that will pass [government] inspection, shake loose of these folks hangin' on me, and fly to freedom [laughs loudly].

Ruby's hopes and dreams have little likelihood of fulfillment. Her life is immeshed in the welfare syndrome, but she has somehow successfully raised most of her eight children, and through her children she finds hope. Admonishing them to avoid the pitfalls of her life, she tells her girls, "Get youself straight, don't follow me, don't let no man drag you down."

Indeed, the whole younger generation in this household, growing up with a mixture of traditional and contemporary values, seems confident and assured of a better life.

CHAPTER 10

Leroy and Rose McCoy

The Welfare Elite[1]

Driving up to the McCoy residence is like looking for the office at a junk yard. Set apart from the other houses on the street, its ample yard has become the graveyard for a white Fleetwood Cadillac, 1970 vintage, a mid-seventies golden Chrysler LeBaron, several battered pickup trucks, as well as a quantity of furnishings, overstuffed chairs, television sets and a washing machine. Playing among these ruins are perhaps a half dozen children from diapers to near teens, who have in turn surrounded themselves with bicycles in assorted sizes and toys of every description. This is the largest welfare family in town, incorporating three generations with just the right credentials to maximize public support. Leroy McCoy, the patriarch of the family, is a rotund middle-aged man with graying beard and an ever-present baseball cap to cover his balding head. Like the town elders, he is an inveterate porch sitter. With a bowl of snacks at his side, he sits for hours yelling frequent directions and admonitions to the children at play. Many years ago he decided it wasn't in his nature or best interests to answer the six o'clock sawmill whistle every morning. Declaring himself retired at forty, he sent his wife off to El Dorado to find work in a restaurant,

[1]Many superficial details describing this family have been altered to protect their identity.

employment that she has kept to this day, while he pursued more creative outlets for his energy and wit. His next order of business was to advise the welfare office that his withdrawal from the work force was due to ill health (his obesity had, in fact, resulted in high blood pressure and an irregular heart rhythm), leaving his large family with only his wife's meager income. His household of eight children quickly qualified for maximum A.F.D.C. and food stamps, amounting to nearly $600 per month.

Leroy liked to fish, and before long, always short of ready cash, he added a few nets to his fishing tackle and concentrated on catching large catfish and buffalo carp to sell around town. His cash business thrived and in no way interfered with his official "no visible means of support" designation at the welfare office. His family was delighted when Leroy had found work pulling in $100-200 per week much of the year and established himself as a regular vendor in Calion, selling fish up and down the streets from the back of his pickup truck. In an expansive mood on his porch he often advised the less fortunate to give up their heavy labors and go in business with him.

Meanwhile, his industrious wife, who had borne him no less than nine children from her early marriage at fourteen, was still young and vigorous enough to keep their large household together, doing almost all the cooking, washing, and cleaning single-handed. At the same time she held down a full-time job as a short-order cook uptown. Rose was remarkable, a handsome woman, large and robust with a sunny disposition that by all reckoning was sorely tried by a demanding home life. With such a melange of children in every stage of growth, her weekends were often spent in the emergency room at the hospital where everything from a runny nose to a broken arm was professionally cared for under the family's Medicaid qualifications. Undeterred by long hours at work, Rose seems always at the vital center of her household, which still includes five of her own children plus three of her children's children, all of whom were born out of wedlock to her teenage girls. Their house, relatively small, is literally packed to the walls with children: Rose's own minor children ranging in age from eight to sixteen years; and in addition, her daughters' three, aged two months to two and one-half years. The sixteen-year-old, Helen Jean, in circumstances common in Jelly Roll households, became pregnant by an unaccounted-for father, and chose not to have an abortion, giving birth and bringing the baby home to her mother, then returned to high school. Leroy comments, "they drop these little surprises on us like they was givin' us a Christmas present."

Helen Jean, not a particularly attractive young girl, short and overweight, nonetheless became sexually active and "popular" when she was thirteen, began drinking and smoking marijuana, and for a while ran with the older high school crowd. her mother openly states that she "turned off hateful and flat out'a control" as a teenager until she got pregnant, and since then "has quieted down some and not become pregnant again." Helen Jean has returned to high school but is not passing, her attendance is erratic and she is also away from home for days on end. Now she remembers her baby only at birthdays and on Christmas, an increasingly foreign object from her past, a ward of grandmother and the state.

In Jelly Roll the sharp drop in second pregnancies, where the young father and mother do not form a household, suggests that, once having starred in the big event, more sobering forces come into play. Many girls explain that subsequent attention to birth control depends on parental reaction to the first child. Rose and Leroy both publicly and privately bemoaned the advent of more children into their already overcrowded home, despite added A.F.D.C. support. Nevertheless, they did not hesitate to take the babies in, as they did Helen Jean's, and appear to lavish more affection and attention on them than their own children in true grandparental style. But these babies are also a frequent source of conflict betweent the generations as the role of "little mother" is alternated with teenage school girl. Subsequently, under conflicting pressures the child is often given over totally to the care and responsiblity of the grandmother.

Moreover, the romance of motherhood is seldom matched by a knowledge of its mechanics. Many young mothers express their surprise and shock at the pain and trauma accompanying even a perfectly normal first birth and later give this as their reason for resorting thereafter to proven techniques of birth control. There is also a pattern here, more likely when older teenagers become pregnant, to quarrel with parents and form their own separate households; in fact, pregnancy can be a means of escape from an unhappy home, but this calls forth a law as old as man's primitive heritage: "no new hunter, no new household." Its modern equivalent still pressures the young father to find a job, usually by dropping out of high school into the precarious unskilled labor market. This road to family formation is fraught with pitfalls, There are infinite variations on its failures, but each incorporates certain hard facts of life in America today that include the lack and impermanence of unskilled jobs, the absence of public transportation and related problems of commuting, deficiencies in education and faulty skills attributable to public school diploma mills, and lack of home and external conditioning for the demands of successful employment. This last factor is most telling, for even in a small town such as

Calion without significant unemployment, youth is often uninformed, antagonistic or too easily distracted to conform to basic job market requirements of punctuality and reliability.

Such a syndrome of failure is typified in a domestic episode involving Rose McCoy's eldest son Sammy Joe. Their story starts out promisingly enough. Sammy Joe and his girlfriend of several years, Ida Cole, were both concluding the first semester of their high school senior year when Ida became pregnant. Since they were both very much in love, they decided to get married. Sammy would get a job and finish high school at night, and Ida, a superior student, would have her baby and then go on to a technical school in computer technology. Sammy got an entry-level job in the lumber yard at Calion for a little over five dollars per hour, and all signs pointed to success for the young couple. But Rose openly blamed her new daughter-in-law for letting herself get pregnant and thus preventing Sammy Joe from finishing school. Moreover, Ida, the youngest of three children, was an "uptown girl" whose parents both worked, owned a large home in El Dorado, and, as Sammy says, looked down their noses at his family with all their personal turmoil.

Sammy, whose capital had never amounted to much more than a twenty-dollar bill, wanted to rent a place in Calion near his parents and near work, putting distance between his little family and his mother-in-law. His own parents could have provided the $400-500 it would have taken to cover an advance month's rent, utility deposits and a minimum down payment on a few used furnishings. Unfortunately, their baby came at Leroy's off-season for fishing, so this, coupled with Rose's coolness, left the young couple with no alternative other than to bring the baby home from the hospital to Ida's parent's house until Sammy and Ida could save enough money to move out on their own.

Problems surfaced almost at once when Sammy, without a car or the means to purchase one, had to catch rides with unreliable friends to his job at Calion. This led to absentee days, lost incentive pay, a missed promotion, and finally a punitive layoff for a week. Things were going no better at home where the ancient brew of son-in-law versus mother-in-law was working its chemistry of alienation. By now having found a good drinking buddy with whom he could commute, Sammy came home later and later from work. Finally, after one more violent scene with his wife and her kin, he left or was thrown out of their home. Ida was to remain in the warm lap of her family, now eligible through the abandonment of her husband to obtain $300 plus per month in A.F.D.C. and food stamps for herself and her infant child.

In the meantime, Sammy had lost his job but found shelter in the arms of an older woman who held a good supervisory job at the local poultry processing plant. As they say on the streets, Sammy Joe became "a roamin' stud," living off first one woman then another, hanging around bars and carry-outs, beer in hand, with only the briefest subsequent forays into the job market. This pattern can and probably will continue as long as he is young enough, clever enough and still attractive enough to be a kept man, "a Sonny Boy." After that his future becomes most uncertain. Ida, on the other hand, with home support, government aid and her young life still ahead of her, has more viable options.

Eighteen-year-old Natalie McCoy is a tall, handsome young woman with a flair for clothes, a good singing voice and a thwarted ambition to be a popular musician. But Natalie had her first pregnancy at fourteen as a result of a brief affair in high school with a classmate, Bobby Lee Smith. Although torn by their decision, both Leroy and Rose urged their daughter to have an abortion because of her youth and frail health. But Natalie adamantly refused; "If I'm woman enough to get one, I'm woman enough to take care of one," she exclaimed again and again in the face of opposition. It was a difficult pregnancy, including kidney complications and enforced bed rest, culminating in a prolonged labor and the premature birth of a baby boy. The long ordeal had somehow raised the entire McCoy household to a fevered pitch of excited activity and preparation, belying the presence there already of so many children. In recalling the event Natalie still glows, "That little 'tater made me so proud and happy. After all, if I weren't takin' care of my own, I'd be takin' care of someone else's now, wouldn't I?"

Early on, the gravity of events frightened off the young father, and Natalie fell back upon the support of her mother, who stood by her during the long repeated trips to the hospital and willingly gave the subsequent special care required for the mother and tiny infant. After missing a semester, Natalie was able to return to high school and graduate, while Rose kept the baby and her welfare check. However, after graduation, much to her parent's chagrin, Natalie took up with Bobby Lee again. For a while they lived with his mother in El Dorado, enduring all the expected complications. When Natalie announced to her family that she was pregnant again, her father Leroy sprang into action. He found the young couple an old rent house in Calion and set them up in housekeeping. His aid coupled with a modest loan that Bobby secured from the lumber company, where he was now an employee in good standing, made the move a complete success.

The young couple seems to be settling into the routines and responsibilities of married life, despite the usual bones of contention over money and Bobby's too frequent nights out with the boys. "Why can't he stay home and do right?" Natalie laments. "No good'll come of drinkin' and hangin' round those joints. He must think he's still a stud or somethin'." When a Saturday fishing trip turns into a late night drinking bout, or when they fight over who is spoiling the children, and whether to buy a car or a better refrigerator, it is then that Natalie thinks nostalgically of a missed career. Having enjoyed some success and praise in high school musicals, she had at one time harbored serious aspirations of becoming a singer. She feels that her frequent fights with Bobby have squelched much of her earlier vivacity. She is bored with the long days of child care and soap operas at home, the tedium seldom interrupted by more than daily walks to her parents' home when the weather permits.

Bobby Lee, on the other hand, is having an equally difficult time settling down to "one beer and one woman," when many of his high school cronies are still at large. The glamour on the streets is still in his eyes, and he seems shocked and hurt by Natalie's violent reactions to his little junkets. Yet, all in all, their marriage appears to be succeeding. Bobby is a steady worker and a devoted father, but like Natalie does not want any more children. "This is one time a pair beats a full house," he laughs. Unlike Sammy Joe and Ida they had received critical financial support from family and job at the crossroads of their relationship.

And the role of welfare? For Bobby and Natalie it eased their financial problems during the difficult period of household formation with infant children to support. Following Leroy's sharp, if unethical, maneuvers, the couple purposely did not marry, nor did they advise the welfare people that there was a wage earner in the house. Hence, Natalie continued to receive their welfare check and food stamps at Leroy's address. As long as the authorities don't learn the truth, Natalie and Bobby have a comfortable supplemental income. Since Bobby is well established in his job and brings home the primary check, this has not overturned his position as the head of the household. In fact, when last interviewed the young couple were looking to the time when they would be "turned in by some no-count troublemakers" but felt no guilt about bilking the government out of $300-plus dollars a month. Rather, they viewed this money as an American entitlement, a white man's ransom for years of slavery and discrimination that might soon be wrenched from their hands. In any case, with Bobby's improving job prospects, his wages over $250 per week, they could now be judged as capable of easily riding out the shock from losing all welfare benefits.

An overview of the McCoy family and its three generations is revealing. Leroy and Rose were married over twenty years ago and set up a dynamic, family-oriented household that still remains at the center of the lives of their nine children and many grandchildren. Of the nine, only one has officially gotten married and three of their children away from home are also receiving welfare. The senior McCoys, thoughs still active and enterprising, receive welfare for five children remaining at home. Their somewhat battered house is equipped with all the modern conveniences and gadgetry. There are two family cars and a pickup truck. The family eats well, takes short recreational trips and dresses in the latest styles. The McCoys are, in fact, no less than welfare elite. They are also welfare cheaters: Leroy is engaged as a fisherman in the underground cash economy, a crime no better nor worse than doctors or plumbers who exchange work or take in unreported cash receipts. Like Leroy, whose welfare assistance goes back twenty years, his children have learned to play the system for all that it is worth. There are times when the family would have been hard pressed without it, especially their Medicaid coverage during many pregnancies; but the overall impression that one gets from any interviews within this family conglomerate is one of vigorous viability.

The McCoy family demonstrates once more that the fruits of the welfare tree are easily picked, and punishment for breaking the rules seems rare and remote, seldom striking close to home. For in the final analysis, the welfare system, like the undercover cash economy, defies effective enforcement.

CHAPTER 11

Saphire and Wilbur Hines

Home is Like a Honky Tonk

The Hines live conveniently at the end of the street on a large lot adjoining a shady creek lined with feathery cypress trees and a thicket of small oaks. Their large trailer house faces the creek, not the street, and has a spacious living room that opens out onto a raised wooden deck. By chance or by design, the setting is perfect for the life style of its owners, a gregarious couple who have allowed their home to become a sort of club for their friends and neighbors.

As one approaches the house early on a sunny Friday afternoon, four or five cars are probably already parked in the ample yard. A few people, sitting on buckets and in lawn chairs, loiter about the cypress grove by the creek exchanging casual conversation and sipping the inevitable tall can of beer. Moving toward the deck the group is larger and the conversation louder and more animated; while, on the inside through the open screenless door, four or five are seated at the dining room table where they have started up an early two-bit game of black jack. Outside against the wall on the shadiest part of the deck Saphire herself sits, looking alternately stern and jolly as the conversations ebb and flow around her. Practically everyone has a beer can in hand which, when drained, will be pitched unceremoniously into the yard adding to the already sizeable accumulation. Periodically Saphire's father will collect the cans, crushing them with a quick stomp of the heel before placing them in plastic garbage bags for future sale. Saphire explains that these bags of cans are her "savings account" to be cashed in an emergency, as when beer money gets dangerously low.

Saphire, a formidably large and corpulent woman, presides at these gatherings much like a Polynesian queen over her court. Although extremely overweight, she is nonetheless a strikingly handsome woman of thirty whose full features still reveal a youthful beauty. Her dark, penetrating eyes register her changing good humor. Her husband, Wilbur, five years her senior, is a strong but acquiescent consort. He is a leader and a skilled employee at the sawmill. Thin, on the quiet side, and mostly in the background, he forcefully inserts himself into the proceedings only when a visitor gets out of line or the company becomes to raucous. The Hines have five children, three young boys aged eight, nine and eleven, and two girls, thirteen and fourteen. Exuberant in their youthful beauty, the girls are deferred to by all and, under the watchful eyes of their parents, are frequently attended by a roving troupe of teenaged boys.

Saphire was a middling child from a large Jelly Roll family. Her mother is recently deceased, but her father like her husband works at the mill and lives just several houses away. He is close to his daughter and her family and, since his wife's death, drops by to visit regularly. He fondly recollects times past when his own home was also a gathering point. Now his daughter proudly maintains the family tradition. Saphire, pregnant with Wilbur's child, dropped out of school after the ninth grade. Her daily routine of "lazying around the house" and never straying far from home became set after that first pregnancy. By her own admission she has many anxieties about traveling, even by car to nearby El Dorado. She has never worked, rarely traveled and seldom even crosses the street to her father's house or to visit neighbors. Wilbur does all of the grocery shopping himself; but at home, Saphire reigns supreme over her family and her court, consisting of kinsmen, friends and freeloaders, as well as many town youth who have fallen under her spell.

One day is very like another. Some court regulars arrive as early as mid-morning to partake of an eye opener, the first beer of the day. Inventories are assessed and fresh provisions ordered. On a warm day the assemblage follows the sun, moving from the yard to the deck to the air-conditioned living room as the day progresses. There is usually a steady coming and going of friends and card players. After three in the afternoon when the school bus lets out their five children, youths of all ages are added to the mix, prominent among whom are the girl's young suitors who idle about or rough house in the spacious yard.

Beer is the offical beverage here, but Saphire and her favorites partake from time to time from quarter-pint bottles of bourbon stowed conveniently in Saphire's handbag. Although the routine dress of the assemblage is work clothes casual, the grounds but a dirt yard and the residence an aging trailor house, there is here an unmistakable air of a select gathering.

Although in these times the unrelenting pursuit of pleasure is not uncommon, still it is unusual to make one's home into a social club for a good segment of the community. Despite the incessant comings and goings of wanted and unwanted guests, the Hines are defiant and proud of their establishment and their role in the community. As Wilbur explains it:

> People don't have any place to go in Calion except to the lake [beer emporium], where there's lots of fights and trouble's waiting for you. We give them a place to go where they can have a beer, visit with each other and, yes, play cards without getting into trouble. . . . We were a big family in Hampton. I worked on a farm, stayed so much apart from people that I really looked forward to our family get-togethers. Mother taught me to treat everybody nice, respect people; and I expect them to respect me. I don't clown around with them, so they hear me good when I say something or send them on home with a 'See you tomorrow.'

Saphire is equally sure of her role as a neighborhood attraction. She knows who she is and exactly what she is doing:

> I draw people to me. It's just natural. I'm not tryin' to collect all these people you see around here. I really like to be by myself a lot of the time. Sometimes, I'll go into my room and lock the door. Sometime, I lock the front door, and I won't answer it if you knock, sometimes for days. . . . It's always been crowded around me like this, even before we lived in this big place; everywhere I have stayed in Calion, I've always had lots of company. Wilbur is a real friendly person, too, so you see, people must like being with us. Friends bring me beer or a half pint, and we get to talkin'. For some reason, people want to tell me their troubles. Maybe you'll come to me with yours some day. . . .
>
> I don't like to leave this yard, even to go see Daddy. I don't have to leave, people come to me. I don't talk on the streets. People don't know shit about me, but they talk a lot about what they think they know. If you listen to them, stay away from me! Hit my door! Let them mind their own business and quit makin' up tales about what's goin' on over here. . . .

> I most like to talk to the young. They are my best friends — some of them you might call drifters. I talk to them easy like, make them feel good; and I damn sure don't go around gossiping, stabbing people in the back the way they do in this town. That's why people open up to me, tell me things they wouldn't breathe to anyone else. Yeah, I can talk to the young, and I love children. Did you notice how the neighbor's children come runnin' around over here and even call me Mama. I have affection for them, love them like I love my own children.

Saphire does indeed possess a magnetic warmth that is seemingly available to all who would solicit it. There is an uninhibited exchange of affection between her and her children, a rare quality of mutual adoration. As soon as the school bus stops, her children all rush to her, each one coming close to caress or hug their mother, to show her their school work, no matter how many guests and revelers may be gathered around her. In the afternoon, she will sometimes sit on the sofa with her arms around her two teenage daughters, fussing with their hair, whispering little personal things to them. The girls exchange anecdotes from the day's happenings at school, then volunteer their plans for the afternoon to their mother, a far cry from the typical teen-parent confrontations.

The children, both boys and girls, have a more formal, less tactile relationship with their father. Since he alone acts as disciplinarian, he also receives on occasion their rebellious hostility. But their mother is all permissiveness. She prides herself on her relationship with her children as friends, the objects of her affection and amusement. Even the youngest are treated as quasi-adults in a crowded adult world in which there is no attempt to shield them from unexpurgated adult humor, profanity, boisterous carousing, amorous advances or the constant temptations of liquor. Saphire professes to be unconcerned about any negative effects this environment might have on her children's lives. To the contrary, she views it positively because, "Life is tough, and the sooner they learn about how it really is, the better."

The Hines' life style is casual in the extreme. The children seem to drift about house and yard without chores or a mandate to help out in any way. No one seems concerned about washing dishes that remain all day in the sink; cleaning and straightening seldom occur. Saphire is indifferent to discipline, consistently treating her children as friends and confidants, much as she treats the adults close to her. "I tell them anything they want to know. No secrets. It's useless to hide the truth from children." Wilbur concurs. In fact, nothing much can be hidden in this social environment. But the Hines formula is based upon love, caring and presence. Saphire is always there, always has time. She is ever consoling, counseling and stroking her brood. This ever-present concern seems to override the cigarette smoke, beer cans and loud guests; through it all the children appear to be growing up whole and relatively unscathed, although such a judgement may be premature.

Liza, the oldest daughter, has a regular part-time job at a nearby restaurant, though she is fourteen. Both girls go to church regularly, but the boys do not. So far, as Wilbur puts it, "The kids have kept their noses clean."

The Jelly Roll community's appraisal of this family is distinctly divided between loyal supporters and severe critics. The more conservative, church-oriented townfolk, young and old, view the Hines establishment as little less than Satan's den. Saphire and Wilbur are sharply criticized for running a gambling joint, corrupting youth and permitting their children to run wild. However, in all fairness, one would have to say that the jury is still out on their case. Few disturbances have arisen from their popular congregations, and the children, while spirited, independent and street-wise, have so far stayed clear of serious trouble. Their daughters, although precocious, have not yet come up pregnant, and no one is failing school. The home atmosphere, sometimes made raucous and raunchy by their guests, remains one of love and solicitude under the concerned eyes of parents. The children are urged to succeed but not to excel. Finishing high school is their highest goal, along with making a good pay check and living the good life.

CHAPTER 12

Low-Profile Mainstream Families

The lives of more traditional families seem less dramatic and uneventful when compared to the high profile minority of welfare matriarchs, street studs or colorful old timers; for they are the less conspicuous working people of Jelly Roll's citizens. They are a majority of the community's households, but just barely. As a group they are most likely to include those who have formed stable families, have regular employment, neither ask nor receive welfare in any form and support the local churches with their contributions and their presence. They are also inclined to champion education, sending most of their children through high school and occasionally college without frequent mishap; and they venerate past traditions through a certain degree of emulation and respect for the values of the old folks. Although this majority covers the gamut of individual differences, their problems and traumas, fears of pleasures tend to parallel those in the broader category of working-class America. While retaining some venerated black traditions and identity they have also moved perceptibly into the mass media society of contemporary America.

Tommy and Mable Plunkett

The Plunketts, both in their mid-forties, married for twenty-six years, are a well-settled, industrious family with five children.

Mable is third generation Jelly Roll, and the house in which they live was built by her mother's parents, both of whom lived past their hundredth birthday. Her father and maternal grandfather had lived, worked and retired at the mill. Her husband, Tommy, came from a nearby farming community and worked for a butcher for a brief period in Norphlet before also going to work at the Calion mill.

The work ethic is the centerpiece of this family's life and routine. Tommy is a steady worker who stays close to home and job, walks the street for recreation when he is not off squirrel hunting alone, and is prone to a few too many beers on weekends. But the family mainly revolves around the customarily seated figure of Mable Plunkett in the living room near the never-darkened television set. Here chores, mending, hairdressing, homework and snacking busily progress while watching and commenting on TV serials or movies that mark the passage of the hours. Mable's ample frame is cornered on the black vinyl sofa directly opposite the TV set, and it is from here that she directs both traffic and commentary on the life and times of her family.

> I've worked all my life since I was a little girl helping my mother after my father had back surgery. When I graduated from high school I went to work for Dr. Winslow's family. He was such a beautiful man! He was so sad when I told him I was gonna quit and get married. 'You're committing suicide,' he said. He tried to change my mind, even offered to help send me to college. But no. I had to go and get married like the young fool. Right there I spilled the milk and I've been mopping every since. I've worked at the hospital, nursing homes, your furniture plant and now I got this graveyard shift as watchman at the refinery. My back won't let me take those heavy lifting jobs. . . .
>
> I'd never get married again. Things change after you're married. Tommy and I don't do things together like we used to. But I put disappointment behind me and go on. Me and my children have to do whatever gets done around here. We split up the burden. Believe me, it's detrimental to a woman not to have a handy man around the house.

Mable makes no bones about the fact that she and her husband have drifted apart emotionally through the passing years. But the vitality and viability of this family is undisturbed by real or imagined differences.

Quietly and assuredly Mable directs her four children living at home in their various housekeeping tasks. Their oldest, Tommy, Jr., age twenty-five, is a career Army man now stationed in Germany; their oldest daughter, Linda, twenty-two is doing the laundry while Shirley, twenty-one, prepares for her evening classes in

Secretarial Business at the El Dorado vocational school. Fourteen-year-old Elmer is sent off on errands to the store and the post office while youngest daughter Dinah, eleven, sits on the floor at her mother's feet patiently enduring the tussle to undo the corn-row braids in her hair. The conversation revolves around the chitchat concerning school, jobs and home. Eyes are fixed on the TV soap opera that periodically evokes comment and excitement, for television provides a constant, moving backdrop to their domestic lives. During a lull in the action, Dinah is dispatched to the carryout for a quart of ice cream which, upon her return, everyone devours eagerly. Mable explains that although she and her daughters are good cooks, their varying schedules leave them hungry at different times. Consequently, eating has become an individual matter, snacking, making sandwiches at all hours or ladling out of a large pot of beans on the stove. "We only sit down together on Sundays," Mable laments. "If it weren't for church, this family would never pull itself together."

When the two younger children are gone from the house, it is only for short periods of time; they check in with their mother regularly for instructions and new chores. Mable picks up the account of their lives:

> Our house burned down three years ago, and we moved in with my grandmother here in this house. She was ninety-eight then, a little lady still fit and very independent. She drew her own bath and washed her own clothes by hand since she believed the machines tore them up. I was always under her spell. She was a dominant woman, and 'Paw Paw,' my grandfather, was a very quiet man, like my husband. Grandma kept everything ship shape, inside and out, did the yard herself until she was almost a hundred years old. . . .
>
> I can remember walking miles to church at Champagnolle with Mother and Grandmother. As we got closer we all got excited. You would feel the Spirit before you ever made the church house yard. Even before the singin' and the prayin', you knew what God was all about. But now it seems like the more God blesses us, the less we want to praise him. Grandmother had made me practice the piano for two and a half hours every day until the day I married, so I got pretty good. I've played the piano at church for many years. I make my kids go every Sunday. I've told them when I look back from the piano that I want to see them there. I gave Elmer the choice to sing in the choir or usher, and he chose to usher. Some of his so-called friends poke fun at him, try to laugh him out of church because they don't go. There are some people on the street that don't want

to do anything worthwhile. They have junkie minds! Now they walk the street looking for a handout. Our pastor says we should practice what the Bible preaches and help them no matter who they are. But I can't see it. I've got arthritis but I go to work in pain. Why should I come home and feed these no-count street people? I told the preacher, 'You keep your Bible, and I'll keep my opinion and refuse the opportunity to care for these ripoff triflers.'

I've tried to raise my children to be independent. Get an education so they can make it on their own out there. Linda made a terrible mistake when she married this Williams boy in this Army uniform when she was just sixteen. She stayed with him for three miserable years though he never supported her right. Finally I told her, 'Get a divorce and forget this dude, because you're going to have to be your own bread winner.' Well, she did it. Got her mind straightened out, graduated from high school, joined the Army reserves, and got a job at the chemical plant while she's getting her vocational school degree as a business secretary. Linda got it all together. She spends wisely, has done all the shopping for her family since she was fifteen, and is a good cook to boot. Really, she's just an all-around girl. I'm proud of her, but then I'm proud of all my kids.

Henry and Donna Walters

They are a young couple in their late twenties, an industrious pair with three children ages six to ten. Both work, he at the sawmill, she at the furniture plant. They live in a well-cared-for company-financed mobile home but want a bigger place and more land. Henry wants to do a little farming, and Donna wants enough yard to avoid the prying eyes and ears of neighbors. Henry is assistant pastor at the Shady Oak Baptist Church and is also pastor of a small rural church with a congregation of just four families. He is an intense, ambitious young man with a restless spirit and a will to succeed:

I have to work at your mill to make a living, but I know I had the calling to the ministry when I was shot through the head, right above the eye, back when I was on the police force. I had brain surgery, and they put a steel plate in my head. If I survived that, I can bear whatever comes, right?

I lost my first church, but I was young and inexperienced preachin', and I didn't know about getting hooked up with a one-family church. I bucked the head lady and lost. I knew a little about church work, but not enough about black folks.

My people have a nice little farm out of Fordyce. My

father is a church deacon, and there are three ministers on his side of the family. I moved to Calion because Reverend Bradford wanted me here as his assistant. He's encouraged me and helped me in every way he can. My wife is head of the Sunday School program, and she is full to overflowing. Reverend Bradford has taught me a lot. He's not one of these whoopin' and hollerin' kind. He uses the teaching style of preachin', and those that understand swear by him. Some people say that I can't preach, but I'm learning his way and there is so much to learn. . . .

I went through high school, but I didn't apply myself, barely passed when I could have been making A's. But I had other things on my mind, if you take my meaning. I've knocked around a good bit. I took electronics in vocational school until it got so hard that I had to start dating the teacher to pass the course. Listen, I've been working since I started carrying slabs in a peckerwood sawmill at thirteen. After I quit vocational school, I worked in a service station. Enjoyed meeting the public. Then I took a job as an orderly in a hospital in Louisville, Kentucky. My first wife and two children still live there. When she divorced me, I lost twenty-one pounds grieving over losing my precious daughter. We still talk all the time over the telephone. Another big expense!

My second wife is a good woman. She's not a complainer, happiest when she's workin'. They still call her to come back to the nursing home, but she's working here in Calion to please me even though she's really a city girl.

We're strict with our children, and we're strict with the kids at church. Any child I'm responsible for, I'm going to keep in line, whip them if they need it the way my grandma did me. If the parents don't like it, they can keep their children at home. When you ride your truck up and down these streets, can't you see the potential young criminals? Only home and church can save them. . . .

Me, I'm trying to find myself spiritually. I want more than a house, a TV and a pile of tin cans at the back door. I needs some land to farm and a good big frame house where I can raise my children along with the chickens and pigs. Then, maybe I could concentrate better on the Lord's business. I'm not afraid of work. My wife and I have so many dreams. . . . Believe in yourself and the Lord, and you can make it happen.

Randall and Mae Jefferson

This middle-aged couple lives in a slumping, odd-shaped house that looks rather like several smaller houses imperfectly nailed together. There is a problem at once to figure out which door to knock on. Upon finally entering, one is surprised by a large, open and well-furnished interior. There is a large living room, a food counter and kitchen combination to accomodate what was at one time a family with eight children at home.

Randall, who was born and raised in Jelly Roll, married his youthful sweetheart, also a local girl, who had her first child by him when she was only fifteen. "After the first one, they seemed to come every year or two. The Lord regularly blessed us, and we took what he sent without a complaint," says Randall, who doesn't believe in birth control, not on religious grounds, but rather from a fatalistic attitude with an added touch of machismo. "Mae never would do anything to keep from having 'em, so we had 'em, and that's it. I've worked hard on that lumber yard all my life, and all I have to show for it are these children of mine."

The Jeffersons have spent their lives committed to the work ethic and child rearing. They live very independent lives and have few social contacts outside their church. Neither has ever taken the luxury to travel more than a hundred miles from home. Randall likes to fish a little, and Mae enjoys an evening of church bingo; but their lives have been polarized by the essentials of survival.

Randall, though only fifty-one, clearly shows the signs of a wearing life. With so many children to raise on the wages of a laborer, he took all the overtime he could get at the mill, and then had to run a pulpwood truck after hours and on Saturdays to make ends meet. Now he has a serious heart condition and several years ago had to have a coronary bypass from which he has never fully recovered.

His wife, Mae, who is ten years his junior, after birthing and raising eight children, seems to have gotten her second wind. A year or so after their youngest child was born, she went to work in the furniture plant to augment the family's income. She has worked steadily in the plant for the last twelve years and is presently supporting the family alone, since Randall's health has failed and he lost his social security disability under the Reagan cutback. Mae is a forceful, strong-minded woman who obviously lives for her children:

> Yes, I've had eight of them, and if I say so myself, they're all beautiful, especially my girls. They naturally have been popular with the boys, but we didn't stand for any foolishness or allow any bad characters to hang around. We kept the girls in close. Their social life was through the church and you may not believe it, but they didn't even ask to go where they shouldn't. I sat a lot just talking to them.

> Still do with Helen, who's at the dangerous age of thirteen. I'll never forget what Darlene told me one time, now she's married to an Air Force man and has a baby. Well, years ago she took my hand and said, 'Mama, I'm gonna make you happy and not get pregnant till after I'm married.' I thanked her for it. I still thank her for it. You must respect your children, be open and honest with them so they can respect you. Some parents think they can get by, but you've got to set a good example for them. And if you say you're going to whip them, you'd better do that, too, right then and there, not tomorrow. Like Randall says, 'You got to steady talk your kids though their young life.' We've done plenty of that. We always try to keep together in what we say, Randall and me, even when we disagree. You better keep the kids from dividing your authority or you've lost them.

Randall did not complete grammar school, which limited his advancement at the mill. Sorely conscious of his own lack of education, sometimes bitter about his lifetime of hard work that got him nowhere, he has reacted with a zealous insistence that all of his children finish high school, have a profession or skilled career and get out of Calion. His message has been heard. There are no high school dropouts in this family. Two of the three oldest boys are in the Army, where they are considering a career. The three youngest, Harold, eighteen; Ollie, sixteen; and Janice, thirteen; are still at home in high school, apparently chafing under their parents' authoritarian, if affectionate "old fashioned," regime. Mae is far less confident of their future and her successful upbringing than she was with her older children:

> It's not the same raising these last children, not as easy. We've tried to raise them all the same, but television has done a lot. They see it all on TV. There's no badness that their young eyes don't see. We can't keep them from it, and we can't keep them off the streets. My sixteen-year-old feels he can do what he pleases. He runs with some boys I don't like. No good. I used to be able to choose their friends. People thought my kids were stuck up because we wouldn't let them run with just anybody. We kept them close to home and close to the church house. But not anymore. These young ones are stubborn. Sometimes I try to put them on probation; but if I don't give them a few dollars, I'm afraid, I hate to admit this, but I'm afraid they'll steal it. So what do you do? There's badness on these streets and everywhere you turn. Sure we try hard, but look at what we're up against.

Thoughts of far-off places

Elmo and Angela Sanders

This is without a doubt Jelly Roll's most surburban couple in the sense of attitude, accomplishment and life style. Elmo, a conservative, soft-spoken young man of thirty, is a skilled machine operator in the furniture plant with an income approaching $20,000 a year. He is an officer in the Union Local, has been Secretary and Choir Director at the Willow Grove Baptist Church, and is active in the town's softball league. His young twenty-three-year-old and beautiful wife, Angela, has a good job at a large chemical manufacturing plant in El Dorado, which, together with her husband's paycheck affords this couple a combined income well in excess of $30,000 per year. They are a devoted young couple who were childhood sweethearts. She fell in love with Elmo at thirteen, and except for when she "ran wild while Mama was living separate in El Dorado for a couple of years," there have been no other men in her life. She happily describes her years with Elmo:

> When Elmo's granddaddy died I came out to Calion to the funeral. Afterwards I went home with him to this house where he was livin'. We spent the night together and I've been here ever since. I mean right here. I'd like a nice house, but not Elmo, his roots go right into the ground underneath this old shack. He was born right in that back room there. . . . For a long time after we got married, I just sat around and got fat. Had my baby almost four years ago. No honky tonkin' for us. Places like that are nothin' but trouble for a good marriage. They say, 'You go juke-juke and you'll get your husband took.' We're flat out of it — go to church, go to Mama's, go to town, or play ball. Elmo doesn't like to party. Sometimes we'll see my sister and her husband — play dominoes and barbeque out. But mostly eat in and watch TV. Man, we're mellowed out homebodies! We've been to California twice and Dallas once in the last six years, but we're happy to be right here. After our sweet baby was born, I went to work in El Dorado. I guess I was bored anyway. I've done my turn sittin' around the house. I'd sure caught up on my sleep and gotten as fat as an old sow. As you can see, I'm slimmed down again. Now I only cook light meals three days a week and on weekends we sometimes go out for chicken. . . . My husband's sister and my mother are my best friends. I've always been shy. Mother says I'm sneaky and was always a tattler. I've never seen the need for a lot of friends. With my family, kinfolks, and the people at work, I see all the people I need to see. Really, if I'm not playing softball or watching Elmo play on a holiday or weekends, I like to be by myself — stretch out

on this big couch and watch the folks on TV go at it for a while.

Angela Sanders' quiet, laid-back style and cultured demeanor belie her background as the youngest of eight children born to the volatile Babe Cole, whom we have profiled. Raised in an overcrowded home long on turbulence and short on money, her personal tranquility and gentle self-assurance are a triumph of character over environment. The phenomenon of Angela makes one ponder the old nature-nuture equation. Indeed, self-assurance is a dominant Cole family trait, but added to this we might speculate, has been the sometimes protective shield of beauty and her position as youngest child in the family.

Although Elmo and Angela have been married six years, and together much longer, they have, so far, had but one child, a daughter aged three. They profess to want one or two more. They possess most of the trappings of middle-class comfort and affluence, two late-model vehicles, a large console TV, comfortable overstuffed furniture and a kitchen with all the gadgets. Only the old frame house with a rotting porch and jerry-built additions give some hint as to this couple's modest origins. Elmo was the second oldest of ten children coming from Jelly Roll's largest clan. While the children were very young, his mother left him and his older sister with her elderly parents and moved to California. Consequently, Elmo was raised under the strict conservatism typical of an older generation.

His young life revolved around church and school and in adulthood, work and home:

> You know, I got a beautiful shotgun for Christmas, but I haven't used it yet. I used to like to go deer hunting a lot, but now there are so many careless people in the woods. . . . I need to fix up this old house before I spend another cold winter in it. So far I haven't been able to get title to it from my mother and uncle. We've burned up the lines to both of them in California but so far no deed and everybody's about half mad. . . . I was born right in that back room. My grandmother was the only mother I ever had. My real mother just stayed here a little while, then left for L.A. I don't remember when. Grandmother died when I was thirteen and my grandfather when I was eighteen. He built this house and he taught me a lot, or tried to, but I was young and hardheaded then. I could have learned much more from him if I'd listened good, but you know how kids are. . . . My daughter is smart, doesn't miss anything, but, oh, is she spoiled. Times have changed for kids. I say that and I'm only thirty. I used to go over to my other grandmother's house to play with all my cousins. They had a houseful, but

don't you know they had fun! Grandma could make some kind of biscuits. . . .

My biggest worry in the world is all these bills. You think we've got a lot saved? Nothing! No matter how much Angela and I bring home — out it goes. You've got to have credit these days. Everything you need costs too much and [laughs] the things you don't need, like dancing lessons for our little girl. . . . I'm a one-woman man. No messin' around. I know we'll be together for a long time. We're homebodies. [Sometimes] I'm jealous of the men she sees at work, but I tell myself, you can't keep someone away from someone else. We have to go on trust, like it or not.

PART III

Youth and Pop Culture

The Accelerating Process of Deculturation

CHAPTER 13

Evelyn and Mike Oliver

Youth in Conflict

Evelyn and Mike are a modern young couple, children of the twentieth century. Both in their mid-twenties, they have been married for five years and as yet have no children. They come from large families with whom they maintain casual but continuous ties. Though professing strong backgrounds of religious upbringing and regular church attendance, neither has been to a service since their marriage. Mike, a native of El Dorado, is one of ten children. He is handsome, lean and clean-cut, with an all-American air about him. In conversation he is soft-spoken, deliberate and reserved, his eyes riveted on you when he is speaking.

Evelyn is a heavy-set girl with a cheerful face, frizzy hair and an ebullient personality; one who likes to "make the scene and dig the action." Whether it is a casual gathering at Clara's Sandwich Shop, the beer joint on the lake or just loafin' the streets, Evelyn is a high-profile, gregarious street person who is seldom far from public view. "Hey there, how you doin'?" is her happy greeting to her many friends around town. It is a recurring source of conflict, then, that Mike wants her to stay at home, even when he is at work. "He always want me shining up this place," she retorts. Evelyn has never held a job for long. She claims her nerves won't let her work those monotonous eight-hour days in the furniture plant. Her husband has often pushed her to find employment so that "she can handle her share of the expenses." So far Evelyn has successfully resisted his pleas, but money is a source of constant conflict between them.

That man won't turn loose of no money. I'm always broke, but I'm scared to go for that easy money pushin' grass." Evelyn is very open about the use of marijuana she sees all around town:

> Everybody, I mean everybody is on the stuff around here. Sometimes it's hard to get the good imported kind. I mean like Columbia Gold or Red Bud. Sometimes they only got the home-grown shit, which puts everybody in a bad mood. I know some dudes around here who make as much as $500 a week when the stuff is good. A pound costs five hundred or more, they can double that if they break it down into dime bags [ten dollars] that make about ten joints. But these pushers aren't gettin' rich [laughs]. They smoke it away, have a party, a good time; you see, if you're dealin', people start to hang around your house. They think it's a country club. Eat your food, drink up everything but the ketchup! Figure you made it, so you can play it, understand? Then they'll turn right around and mess up the man that's feedin' 'em. Call the law if he doesn't give them credit. Too risky a game for me. I'm just a bored-to-death housewife [giggles].

The Olivers' house is the snappiest on the block. Mike continues the spit and polish traditions he acquired in the Army. The yard is always manicured and "the car gets a bath as often as I do," he says. The inside of the house has dark draperies, always closed, leather upholstered furniture and a large leather trimmed bar-console in the living room. With the colorful posters on every wall, the interior has a distinct night-club-like appearance. Mike sits erect upon a bar stool in the living room, while Evelyn chatters away. She refers admiringly to Mike's powerful physique; he responds sarcastically about her weight and her refusal to take regular exercise. She talks of cooking; he responds that she has never learned how to fry chicken. He remains silently aloof and warms to the conversation only when he reminisces about his two service years in Japan, a place he apparently enjoyed immensely in his impressionable late teens. The 12:45 p.m. warning whistle blows at the sawmill and Mike silently rises to return to work. Evelyn seems far more at ease when he has gone. She lights a cigarette, pops a beer and confides in me, "Mike hates white people, but he likes light women. Does that make any sense to you? He puts my family down because we're dark. His people don't like me for the same reason." Evelyn reaches for another cigarette; now there are tears in her eyes:

> I won't go to see his people any more. They act like I'm not there. Same thing when his brothers come by the house,

which is too often! You wouldn't believe how ugly they are to me, and I ain't done nothin'. I think they wish that Mike would leave me and get with another girl he used to go with. She's light like them. I think he still sees her. But who cares! He sees so many women. His Mama, she hates my guts, and he won't stick by me, but what the hell, he's still my man. I cook for him. I tell him I don't want to know what he does away from here as long as he give me my lovin', why should I worry about those whores out there, right? But we had a round when I came home and caught him with another woman in our very own bed. I could have started something, but I didn't. I just handed the bitch her clothes and told her to get out of my face. I blamed Mike for pullin' such a dirty deal, he talked her into it, didn't he?. . . . and Mike, he and Mama are always at it, don't never get along. Why won't he even try? She treats him nice enough except when he starts pushin' her, askin' for money or beer. Bad as she sometimes needs a ride to town, and we be ridin' right by her door on our way. But he won't stop for her, not even if she calls out. Well, here I am still tryin' to live with the man. Give me an 'A' for tryin', will you, teacher?

Evelyn went on, scarcely conscious of my presence, as she chronicled the steady deterioration of their marriage:

Can you believe it? Mike's always accusing me of being unfaithful — mostly because of all the people hangin' around the house here; but I told him I'd grown up with all these niggers. I knew them good, and how they messed with every slut in Calion. Do you think I'd fool with them and chance gettin' syphilis or God knows what? Why we were just sittin' round having a few beers, that's all; but, Mike, now he comes home mostly lookin' for a fight. He's real jealous, doesn't want me to have friends of my own. I think he needs to see a psychiatrist and I told him so. Sometimes he won't let me out of the house to go see my own family. He wants me waitin' on him all the time. But when he comes home, he won't stay long, goes out with the boys at all hours. God only knows what that man's about! When he's home he's too tired to make love, but never too tired to go play baseball.

Shortly after this interview, I happened to visit Evelyn's mother and found her in great distress:

Mike's got Evelyn locked in the house with him all day. I've tried to go in but he won't hear of it. I'm so worried about her. He let her out last night just long enough to come here to bum some cigarettes, and he's been beatin' her something terrible. Her eye was all swelled up, and she was doubled over from him hittin' her in the stomach. Last time, she had to go to the hospital. Everytime those kinfolks of his come down from town, there's trouble. They talk so nasty to her, and Mike goes right along. He say we sleep with white men. That night Mike and Evelyn got into some awful fight. That's when she came down to me. But he came after her with a baseball bat, scared the children half to death. Wouldn't say nothin' to me, just dragged her away. Now I'm so worried. He called in to work sick this morning from next door; been in that house this whole day beatin' on my baby.

Last time it happened we called the Sheriff, but she was too afraid to sign a complaint. So nothin' came of it. Next day, to get back at her he drove her to El Dorado and left her hands full of groceries, and he went back to Calion and got with another woman. Why hasn't she left him? You askin' me? I think she want to. She's tired, but he won't turn loose. Sometimes he chokes her till she's layin' on the floor gaspin' for breath. He tells her, 'Don't you ever try to leave me, or I'll kill you.' Evelyn wants to get away to New Orleans to stay with her sister — slip out while he's at work. He never gives her any money even when he's got a pocket full. Spends it on himself and other women. That man just blows it away!

The next day I saw Evelyn, her head hung, walking slowly down the street. I turned the car around to catch up with her and I could see that her face was puffy and bruised. I offered her bus fare to New Orleans to stay with her sister. She replied curtly, "Thanks, but I don't need it, maybe I'll get a lawyer one of these days." And she walked away.

CHAPTER 14

Conversations in the Singles Society

Erma Jean: Dating Strategies of a Single Mother

Erma Jean is thirty-four, husbandless with three children from the ages of seven to sixteen. She lives in Jelly Roll with her elderly mother in a dilapidated rent house, dependent on the combined income of her mother's social security and her A.F.D.C. and food stamps. She is a long-term welfare recipient, having worked only briefly as a part-time employee in the furniture plant; but when this supplemental income jeopardized her welfare benefits, she quit the job and has not sought employment in several years.

She is an attractive, intelligent, always well-groomed woman who "has to stay slim and stay sharp to make a good hustle." At the time of this interview, Erma Jean was "between men," in something of a financial bind, and in a generally agitated state of mind:

> Mama and I owe everybody in this county. I've got hot checks all over town. Man, if I don't put a good hustle together, they're comin' to get me! I don't mind telling you, it's buggin' me. Since Fred and me split, I just haven't been able to put it all together. I've got my hooks out. I'm workin' at it day and night; but I'm not a twenty-five dollar girl. Most of these men can't afford me. Not around Calion anyway. They don't make enough. . . . I drive to all these little out-of-the-way honky tonks that are fifteen miles or more away from here. I'll sit at the bar talkin' friendly, laughin' with everybody. Pretty soon somebody will buy

you a drink, then another, get you a sandwich, give you two dollars for the juke box to keep it steady jumpin'. Most of the time I only have to put in a quarter or two, and can pocket the rest. I pick up as much as twenty bucks a night that way. . . .

I like the little joints set cozy-like back in the woods out of the way. You'd be surprised the men you meet in places like that — church folks, high class. Of course, most of them are married. Hey! That's why they're out in the back woods where they won't be seen. You'd be surprised at who I meet — lots of high-paid types, the kind that don't mind making your car payments if it suits them. Play it cool! Meet them somewhere for a night or weekend. Everybody's my friend when I'm at a joint, but I come alone and leave alone. I travel light. Me, the good Lord, my car and I. We make our own deals, pull us a bone. I let every town furnish its own men [laughs]. Now don't get me wrong. I'm no hooker. I don't go down like these young girls with every old Tom, Dick or Harry that asks. These girls around here trade these Calion men back and forth like baseball cards. They let their name be in the street for twenty-five dollars. Not this girl! I don't have anything to do with these cats around town. It's too close, and all they do is talk about you in the streets. It's bad enough even if you don't do anything. They make up fantasies about you anyway. But sleep with one of them one time, and it's all over town.

Now, one of these preachers here in town could walk down the street buck naked, and the next time they see him it would still be 'Howdy, Reverend So-and-So.' He's still got his name, understand? But all I have to do is have one little party with one of these dudes and forever after they'll say, 'There goes that whore, Erma, I've had her. . . .'

I've had it with these young bucks. They don't want to spend anything on you. Most of them can't talk, don't want anything but a one-night stand. They just want to get in your pants. Shake you up, bang you then buzz off leaving your body aching in every joint. I've got so I prefer older men. Like the song says, 'Men with that easy touch.' Take you out to nice places for lots of talk. Sometimes you just go out and eat a nice meal and don't even go to a motel; just get out of the car and say, 'Baby, that was fine. It was mellow being with you. . . .'

I never bring my men home. I don't want no man around my house. I've tried all that. They start out fine, pullin' their weight, doin' their share. But soon enough they'll go to leaning on you, lying, cheatin' on you. And I can't stand any more of that. Can't take it any more. Have you ever seen a man here? You won't. All I need is a nice friendly fellow to take up these car payments and cover a few bills. Can't you tell I'm a loner? I can't play sister with anybody either. I never hang around with the women. I don't trust any woman. Mama and me stay to ourselves. I was a friend with a sister-in-law once. Close friends. She had my brother, and I didn't think she'd want my man. But I caught them in bed together. You might say I went crazy. Tried to kill her. I tasted her blood, and now you never see me hangin' round with other women. Like they say, 'If you catch two women hand-in-hand, nine times out of ten they've had the same man.' Now, I'll share anything with you, but not the same man. That's why I travel light and travel alone.

Confessions of a Con Man

George Wesley is a thirty-two-year-old bachelor who keeps an apartment but is rarely there. He cruises his shiny late model Oldsmobile up and down the streets of Jelly Roll several times a day. He is popular with the ladies of all ages, a handsome man with a mischievous glint in his eyes, a profuse talker who seems in his element in street society. His defenses are strong, and he is a boldly self-proclaimed con artist, as the following interview clearly reveals:

Well, Mr. Man, so you've come down to Jelly Roll to see what the poor niggers is all about! No need denying it, all you white people are curious about us. Do you think we're like Chinamen or something? My daddy always said, 'Don't trust the word of no white man, unless he's rich, and if he's rich, don't forget how he got that way.' Everybody listened when my daddy talked. He was a first-class con artist, and he taught himself [laughs]. He got full Social Security disability when he was only thirty-eight, and he's still strong as a young bull. He always told me, 'When you go to the welfare office, don't eat a thing that day, just drink a lot of coffee. Let your stomach rumble good and loud, and don't be a fool and get yourself all dressed up in a three-piece suit. Wear your old overalls, but don't smell bad, have 'em washed fresh, or they won't hear you out. If you can't get a disability any other way, go for the mentally disturbed angle. When they refer you to a psychiatrist — they've always got plants and flowers on the window sill — get up and ask to be excused to go to the bathroom, and then come back with a glass of water and start watering the flowers [laughs].' Do I exaggerate? I have't tried that one yet. Do you think I could pull it off?

Since I'm not working for you any more, Mr. Charles,

you might as well know that I never ran my car on anything but your gas back then. Are you mad? Those boys down there are stealing you blind. I don't see how you can make a dollar. You ought to hire me as an undercover agent. I know what's going on here day and night. Do I talk too much? I know how to play hush mouth, too. . . .

You see, I came up on the rough side of the mountain. My daddy worked like hell on a trashy old patch of land tryin' to feed nine children. My mother never saw a day off that I can remember when I was a kid. But Daddy wasn't no ordinary cottonpatch nigger. He was always lookin' over his shoulder to see what was comin', you know what I mean? Well anyhow, when he saw the chance, he got smart and got on welfare, but by then I had already grown up poor. One thing you'll never see me do is farming. I've slopped so many pigs and chickens, I can't even be kind to a dog.

I've footed it all around this country, slept under bridges, thumbed my way from one sorry job to another. Work six months, then get myself laid off, run out my unemployment, then go to work some place else for another six. Maybe you don't believe I can work these white bosses to lay me off instead of firing me, but I can do it. You got to be half and half. Half slouchy and half eager, then you got it made. After a while, they'll lay you off easy like, and you can draw your unemployment and coast to the nearest rest stop [laughs]. . . .

Once I was runnin' three pulpwood trucks with a half-dozen boys workin' for me. That was the top of my business career, but I about got my ass whipped when the crew found me out light-weighting their loads. That's when I went south for the summer [laughs]. You see what a con artist I am! I'm the way all black people had to be to keep the whites from screwing their ass into the ground. . . .

I'm like my daddy, I need to keep up two women — two houses in case one throws me out or there's trouble, then I still have a place to go right? That sounds just like black folks to you, doesn't it? You don't understand our thinking because you can't get inside of us, you see? . . .

I used to carry a sack full of black pepper and snuff. One lick in the eye will give you a terrible burning eyelid. I keep a loaded pistol in the glove compartment of my car, and the latch is good and oiled. . . . My eyes never stop movin' so I can dig the scene good, make my move ahead of the crowd. Poker is my specialty. I love those all-night games. Why shouldn't I? The longer we play, the more I win [laughs]. . . . I don't want to brag, but it takes self-confidence to make it in this old world, don't you think?

Saturday, young and in love

Lenora: Divorced and on Her Own

Lenora Coleman is a tall, willowy, quiet girl of twenty-five from a large Jelly Roll family. She has a permanently sad expression of one who has been often wronged. She is inclined to sit silently in a group and becomes animated only in one-on-one conversations. She drives her own car, lives alone in a small, older and uncared-for house; and since her divorce settlement from her husband two years ago, has had a low-paying job as a nurse's aide at an El Dorado hospital. Her three small children, two by her former husband and one by a boyfriend, have slowly but inevitably been transferred to her mother's home. Her mother is openly unhappy about the matter:

> Lenora had a good man and didn't know it. He never missed a day of work. Didn't drink too much except on weekends, like most of these men folks. He never treated her rough, even when he was drinking. He loved his babies and brought home his paycheck. But one time, just one time, mind you, Lenora caught him foolin' around with another woman. That tore the blanket. There's just no forgiveness about that girl. Things turned rough after that. They started puttin' the kids off on me while they ran around on each other. I think Jerry, that's her husband, wanted her back, still loved her and his kids, but Lenora would have none of it.
>
> She fell in love with one of those dudes at the hospital, and they made one of those love pacts. You divorce your husband and I'll divorce my wife, then we'll get married, cozy like. Well, you guessed it. Lenora got her divorce, but this dude of hers hung on to his wife and kept Lenora hangin' on to him. So now he's got two houses, right? That's the way these bastards like it. Brag on their two houses in the bars and on the streets. . . .
>
> I did everything I could, pleaded with her not to get a divorce. I told her a man can't have much respect for you if he takes you from your husband. Well, he showed out for the snake he really was when he went back to his old lady.

Lenora is now faced with insoluble financial difficulties: housekeeping as a single mother with a low-paying job and only forty dollars a week awarded by the court in child support. She must drive ten miles to work every day and has a large note to pay on her car. Presently the phone is cut off and she is behind on all her utilities, which became exceedingly high in the winter months. Where she had anticipated financial assistance from her boyfriend, there has apparently been little forthcoming. Her mother continues her side of the story:

> Lenora doesn't even take the kids regularly on week-

ends any more. She keeps the child support check and doesn't give me a dime, can you believe it? Their daddy used to come by and take the older one out regular as you please, but he's about quit now that he's tied up with another woman's children. So that's the way it goes, leave the old folks with the kids and the bills. . . .

Lenora's miserable, I know. Now this dude don't see her unless she fixes things up special — cooks a big meal and turns on the soft music. Makes me think about my brother. Whenever he calls me from California, first thing he asks is, 'Honey, is you payin' for it yet? All the girls is payin' for it out here.' That's not far from what's happening here now. Things is crazy. These men want to hold your check. Not me! How much do you get back? You guessed it!

Anyhow, I told Lenora, 'Girl, you ain't doin' no good. You work every day, got a new fifty-dollar dress and forty-dollar shoes, but your phone is dead, your water's about to be shut off, your kids cry when you pick them up, and you're payin' for a man like all these old women have to do.'

What good did I do? Now she's staying wide away from me; mad that I'm gettin' a little welfare check on her kids. I'm the one that's holdin' these kids. I'm the one that ought to be mad. . . .

Oh, I don't know. Lenora's a good clean girl. She works every day. She's just got man trouble. What's wrong with this country? It don't turn out many good men any more.

When I finally got a quiet time to interview Lenora without her mother's presence, I encountered a totally different perception of the same realities. She seemed little concerned about the impositions her children placed upon her mother; and, not unexpectedly, she was extremely defensive about her balky boyfriend. Typical of Jelly Roll was her passive acceptance of the irresponsibility of men:

The only thing I miss about the man I divorced is his pay check, and I miss that a lot. Well, anyhow, I've got to look after myself, that's all there is to it. I've been working since I was thirteen. . . . Nothing ever made me happier than to leave home. Mother was tough, all those kids. She didn't mind whipping you whether you deserved it or not. I was glad to get out of that house and have my own place where I could sleep when I wanted. I never seem to get enough sleep. . . . Mother is always messin' in your business. She makes everything sound worse than it is. My boyfriend helps me out when I really need it. I just hate to ask for anything. I struggle a lot, but I'm making it on my own. Mother wanted me to get on welfare, but I told her I'd rather work. Welfare's not good enough for me! I don't like the way they treat you, the way they look at you. If I listened to Mother, I'd sleep with every man that came along for what I could get out of him. That's not for me. It has to be just right for me. These young guys don't want to help you; they're just lookin' to go to bed with you. But I tell 'em I don't need a place to sleep. I can always go home and sleep with my kids. . . .

Mother's always pushin' me to get married, but Allen's just not ready. He has his own apartment and a good-paying job. I don't want a husband that's gonna be in the streets. Sure, I'd dump him, and marry 'Mr. Right' if he came along. But I don't know him, do you? I already know Allen. He's a good man, but men are gonna take the easy way out.

Moe Munson: Shade Tree Mechanic

Moe is a handsome young man of twenty-eight, a bachelor with his own "cozy pad" in the form of a small two-bedroom trailer house located on an elm-shaded side street. Two old cars and a polished, late model Chrysler Le Baron fill his small front yard. An automobile engine swings suspended by block and tackle from the overhanging branch of a conveniently positioned large sweetgum tree next to the driveway.

I had first visited with Moe here on a bright Saturday morning as he busily and expertly engaged in "putting a ring job" on a motor hanging waist high from that same sweetgum. Despite the greasy nature of his work, he wore a pair of only slightly soiled tan dress pants and a red satin shirt, with a shower cap to protect his hair. Only his hands and forearms bore the brunt of the motor's encrusted grease and carbon. Our conversation proceeded, his work uninterrupted:

That's right, I can work on one of these jobs and only get my hands dirty. Anyhow, the girls have already seen this old outfit [laughs]. 'Hang it high and make it easy,' I say. You won't catch me hangin' over the hood breakin' my back on an overhaul. If you're dancing you don't do it on your knees. Don't you know, a man can make a career out of cars and women [grins]. I love both of them. Are you going to ask me why I'm working in your old lumber yard if I mean what I say? That's what you're thinking!

Well, it's this way. I'm saving up to start my own little garage and be my own boss. I've got to put together about $3000 for a down payment on the old Gilmore station [on Main Street in Calion]. He's been closed down a year and I expect he's too puny to ever open up again. I've had it on my mind a long time. I'd had it bought already except for emergencies. Pussy done changed my plans, like they say.

No kiddin', they [women] can mess you up. Clean you out and walk away. That's their game. [He shrugged off any elaboration of details.]

Now, I'm gettin' smart. Man, I've had it with gettin' ripped off with these chicks, you hear. It's not the first time I've had to draw down my savings at the company — money I needed for a down payment, just to get out of a jam. Now the money's gone and she's gone. And I'm still workin' the lumber yard. Do you know how boring it is? Sticks and boards all the day. Sometimes I think that [four o'clock] whistle will never blow. Work for yourself and punch your own clock. If I had my own business I'd sleep late and work late at night if I pleased. On Saturdays when I'm workin' on cars, I'll look at my watch and I'll swear I won't believe what that dial says. Day gone by like in no time flat.

I believe that everybody needs to do their own thing. Be yourself, right? With me it's just a matter of money, getting a little down payment together before somebody else buys that garage. I know I can make it because I know I'm good with cars. No, I can't get a 'mechanicing' job up town, too many white men, union crap. But I'm gonna get out of that damn lumber yard, you'll see. . . .

I'm wising up. I've got me a nice mama that's paying me [laughs], Hazel Lamar. She's got a fine job on regular at the Cooper Tire up town. Good money and she don't mind spending some on the man she loves! Do I love her? Well, let's say I likes her fine [laughs again]. She's a little older than I'm used to, but she's a lot of woman. Hazel's old man left her for this young chick about a year ago. It liked to killed her when he cut out! I mean tore her up. She didn't date nobody for most of a year, until I came along, that is. We met at a club in El Dorado, where I hang out some. . . .

Hazel got two daughters, ten and thirteen, that need to be watched close. So, with her working full time she moved back to her mama's house when the man left out. Her mama got one pretty brick house, I'll tell you. Hazel's daddy had been with the railroad before he died. Hazel's got a lot of class, man. She's been spending weekends with me here, well, Saturday nights anyway.

Her mama? She's a nice lady, but she's not partial to me. You dig? I'm a man with grease under his fingernails and all that shit. Why these chicks all the time listen to their mamas? Now Hazel and me can't agree on where we gonna live. She won't hear of bringing her girls out [to Calion]. She's scared of Jelly Roll, too fast for them, she says. And she's a Sister of something or other at her church. Besides, my trailer's not big enough for all of us anyway. So, what the hell! I could live at her mama's place fine, lots of room. I can get along with her mama even though the old lady is crabby as hell. Think of the money I'd save! Yes, that's exactly right, I'd have me that garage and be gone from your damn lumber yard in no time flat.

Women! Foul you up, man! Do you think that old lady gonna let me move in? Shit, no! Nothin' I do make her easy. And I've oiled her aplenty. Hazel loves me, her girls are sweet as pie, but her mama be nothin' but a pisspot. Knockin' on me all the time. Maybe she'll have her way and break me and Hazel up. What that old lady is forgetting is how miserable and unhappy Hazel was before she met me. She used to just sit without talkin' when she's really a big talker. . . .

Our interview was broken up when several of Moe's friends drove up in a smoking old Mercury that was in obvious need of his services. "We're calling for the doctor," said one. Moe dropped his other work and our conversation and eagerly began to attack the new challenge.

Several months passed before I returned for a second interview. I found Moe sitting on the front steps of his trailer house. Tools and engine parts were strewn about the driveway from an engine overhaul still in progress:

Boss man, you caught me in an unusual position, resting! It's plain too hot to stay with it long today. You liked to burn me out on that lumber yard this week. We needs more electric fans down there, I'm telling you. . . . Have you seen how much I've saved up at the office? Over fifteen hundred now. I had another five [hundred], but Hazel got in a scrape on her income tax, and when Big Uncle gets on your case there be no excuses, man. Come up with the money or else. They act like Hitler, I'm tellin' you. Well, I ends up coughin' up five hundred to save Hazel's nerves. Yea, that's right, there goes my game plan again. When me and Hazel first started dating nothing would do but for her to pay more than her share. She was always talkin' about helping me save for buying my own garage. Not anymore! Of course, I know the tire company has been on short hours, and her girls are gettin' to the age when they be needing lots of stuff. But that house of her mama's is paid for, and I know for a fact that her Mama gets two checks. The old bitch! Oh, I shouldn't talk like that. Makes me ashamed. But we could be so happy. I know for sure that Hazel needs a man, and her sweet girls are comin' to the age when they need a daddy who can steady watch over them. But what the hell, the old lady is callin' all the shots.

Since this last visit Moe and Hazel have broken up and Moe is back "on the street" dating several younger girls. The garage was sold to someone else. Moe is still working on the lumber yard, still "mechanicing" on weekends, still saving and ever hopeful of having a place of his own.

CHAPTER 15

Talk About Town

A Casual Exchange

Jelly Roll is much involved in gossip and street talk. In a sense this can be seen as a substitute for the sometimes unaffordable diversions and consumer luxuries that so preoccupy the time and energy of middle-class America. In this little communitiy gossip is a staple of everyday life, and even casual street encounters are often charged with intensity and excitement. Personal exchanges are frequently high-pitched and filled with slights and innuendo; and the ever-present hustle injects a note of wariness in conversations, even among friends. Neighbors deal with each other suspiciously for fear of being exploited or abused. Cooperation is, as a rule, confined to relationships within the family, and even there, is often strained by mutual demands. Except for the ostensible work of several church groups, the spirit of community cooperation, pulling together towards common goals, seems to be as dead as the old timers say it is. In its place is a community hustling a buck and individual advantages, but with style and humor.

On a rainy day one can sit in any number of drab living rooms while the host spins out endless tales of intrigue allegedly transpiring all around you. Moreover, cross-referencing the data presented as related to individual events, with very few exceptions, confirms their authenticity and accuracy. In a little town like Jelly Roll, street talk is "in the know," and apparently there is little time for idle speculation. Street accounts are inclined to distort events by the lurid manner in which they are presented; there is a tabloid quality to the news, as well as the telescoping of time to make unusual events appear to be happening in rapid succession, rather than stretched out over a much longer time frame.

The subsequent dialogue was recorded on a warm, sunny day's visit between the street and porches of three nearby houses. The conversants are all middle-aged or older. Their gossip and commentary concentrates on their observations of the activities of the young people that live around them. The talk is laced with hostilities directed at their contemporary neighbors.

Well how you, Miss Lucy?

Well, I'm not much. This rheumatism like to got me down. I need to go see the doctor, but I can't afford it.

Maybe you need to get in the black jack game at Saphire's house when you get your check. Might make you a killing.

I heard they took Halperna's whole [welfare] check the other night.

She came to play and they showed the way!

More money where that came from. She got three checks comin' in every month besides what she gets off her old man. The house is paid for. She always got money on her.

I heard she brought Helen [her sixteen-year-old daughter] with her to the game.

They were playin' and jammin' until three a.m. Mother and daughter side by side.

Got no business with children alongside of them in a game like that.

She got no business doin' most the things she do, but that never stopped Halperna.

I'm tellin' you, she's lettin' those three girls of hers run wild.

That poor old man of hers don't know which way to turn. They fish the money out of his pants pocket with a coat hanger while he's asleep.

[The two women are joined by a third neighbor].

Hey! Who you sisters knockin' on?

Half the town, of course.

I can't get no sleep for the goings on around here. Those young studs hangin' around across the way all the time.

You can't help but watchin' even when it interferes with your sleep, can you, Aunt Sally? [laughter]

What I see is hot pants and no sense.

Did you hear that thirteen-year-old girl of Alma's is in the family way?

You don't mean it! Followin' in her sister's tracks.

Followin' in their mother's tracks to the welfare office.

When we was young, things weren't so crazy.

When we was young, we wasn't that young. These babies are playin' like adults.

No, the church don't snag but a few. Most are right here on the streets doin' whatever they please.

They can't go to church. Reverend Jones gonna bar the door to those toughs.

That 's wrong to shut out them what needs it the most.

Don't fret on it. They're not breakin' down the doors to get in.

How about your nephew, Russell. I hear he's in trouble with the women again.

He's always in trouble over women.

How come some of that romancin' spirit didn't rub off on you, sister?

I was raised right. Besides, a man was made to ask. You can always turn him down nice, if you don't want it.

Askin' fits Russell's personality. Falls for every woman he has a chance with.

I heard that one of Russell's girlfriends uptown sold everything she had in El Dorado. Came out here with her suitcase in her hand lookin' to move in with him. And, bang! There she was staring his wife and kids in the face.

I mean, that man is courtin' trouble all the time.

You wait. Some sister gonna lay a .38 pistol on him directly, and pull the trigger.

Be lots of cryin' and rollin' around at that funeral.

I guess you heard the latest of Sally Jean's tricks.

You mean takin' Fat Albert away from his wife?

Have you seen him? She's melted that fat boy down to skin and bones. Can't find his strength no more.

She's got the power, takes 'em all on.

I think she's a witch. Puts a real spell on these men when she's grinning all that gold.

Leroy, Willie B., John D. Wilson, Sammy, Jr., Robert Wiler, James Alfred, and that white boy at the plant, to name a few.

She's been down those backwoods roads with most of this town.

But her heart belongs to Mary Jane!

Going both ways. She takes the wives from their husbands and the husbands from their wives.

She's a warhorse for sure. Gets them with that pretty smile and good figure. See what you could do, Aunt Sally, if you'd lose some of that weight? [laughter]

I never kissed but two men in my whole life.

Maybe so, but think what else you did for them!

Hush your mouth! What do you know about it?

Take it easy. At least, I never heard about you payin' the boys for it like Ellen Bradley.

Ain't that somethin' the way she's makin' a fool of herself over that young stud.

Yeah. But her husband gonna tear him up.

He's got to get out of the hospital first.

Awful young for ulcer stomach. Guess she gave it to him.

She's not worth it, but don't he love her!

And her fourteen-year-old daughter goin' with a twenty-year-old man! What is it? Don't she care what happens?

Got no sense and don't give it no mind.

I heard where your girl finally got on at the factory.

She's been lookin' for a job a long time. No babies to take care of, nothin' to do but lay up and drink beer.

She's increased her size right smart.

She's proud to be workin'. Likes to be around men on the job.

That jealous husband gonna beat on her some more.

More! He never gonna quit. But now my baby got her own money. He never gave her enough for cigarettes. Says he made it, so he'll spend it.

Now she got that good money comin' in, maybe she'll help you fix up your house.

Hell, she won't even give me a ride to town when they're drivin' past my door. Bought a new color TV, got two cars and steak for supper; and then, if you believe it, come round here beggin' to borrow two dollars from me for gas money.

These young ones forget who their people are, who raised 'em.

We sacrificed for them, but what do they care for us?

My Jane is true. She says, 'Mama, what you need, Mama? I'll get it for you.' But the others, forget it.

Jane's a good girl.

Jane's an old timey girl, not like most.

You're lucky. When my bunch shows up on Saturdays, they bring nothin' but an empty stomach. Clean me out to the last cup of coffee, and then they're gone again.

My Barbara called me from L.A. Said she was takin' a night job and couldn't keep her baby at home no more. And seein' as I had plenty room, wouldn't I take it for a while. I said, 'Honey, don't you go bringin' me no baby. Daddy is old and sick, and my nerves won't take it.' But she's comin' anyhow!

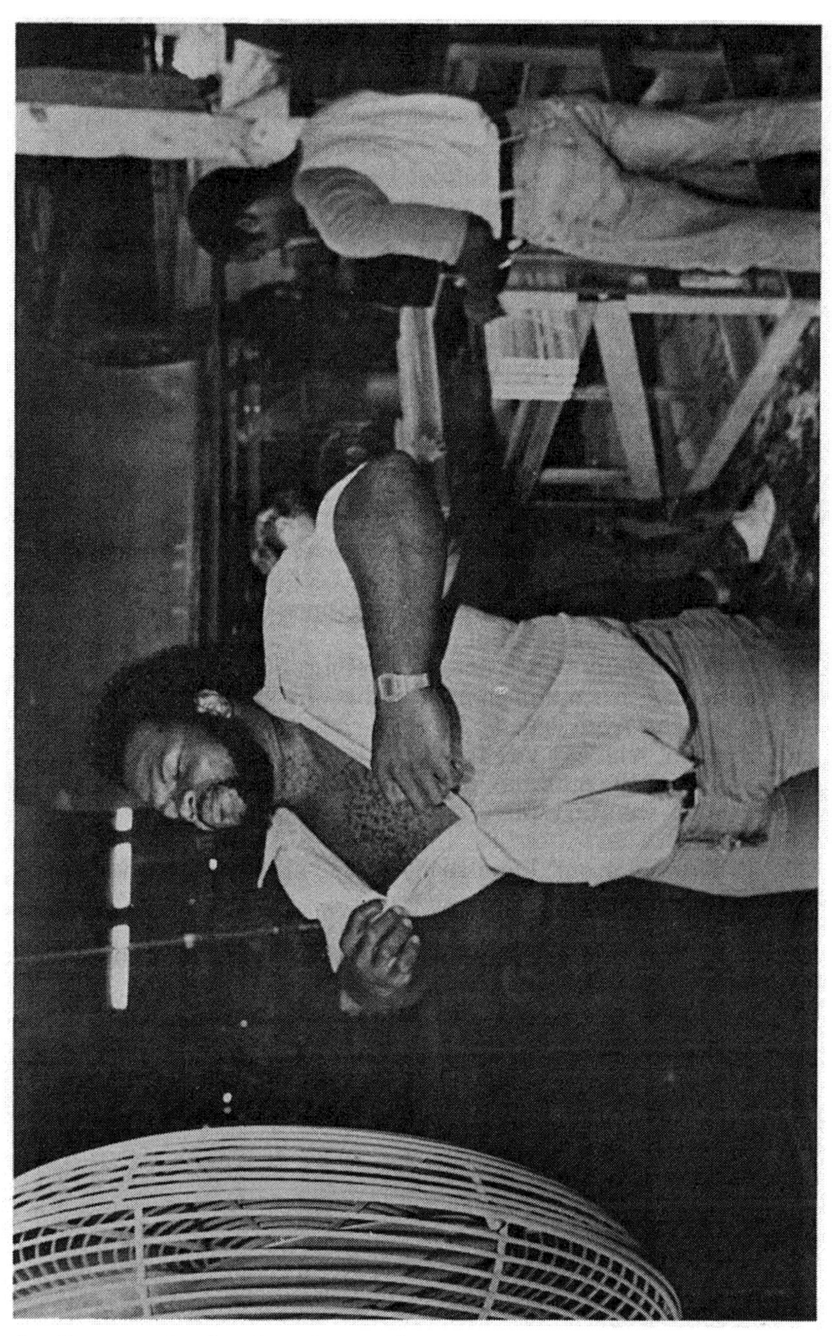

Cooling out in the furniture plant

You gotta be strong, sister; most of 'em around here just cave in and take it.

I don't hear from Barbara except when she got trouble, not even on Mother's Day. Sent me a six-dollar Christmas present.

Did somebody say coffee? I need a cup.

You got some made up, Aunt Sally?

No, I'm fresh out. Let's go to your place.

Well, I'm flat out, too.

Well, I expect I'll be headin' home then, my feets is killin' me.

Guess I'll go and clean up my ugly old house.

When was the last time you got a cup of coffee off Aunt Sally? [laughter]

I'm gonna quit bein' easy and tell that old sister off some day. She'll come over and drink my coffee every day, but try to use her phone and such a fuss you never heard.

She thinks she got that house full of fine furniture and stuff, and we'll pick somethin' up. Never lets you any closer than the porch.

I say you can punch me around some, but don't walk on me. Don't call me a thief.

Aunt Sally's just naturally stingy. So afraid you're gonna beat her out of somethin' that she just keeps taking all she can from you.

Well, who can you trust?

I trust the mailman what brings my check, that's who.

You wouldn't have five on you till the first of the month?

Now, look out! I'm already picked clean from the kids' visit last Saturday.

'No harm in askin', like they say.

Well, I best get back in the house and fix up a pot of beans.

CHAPTER 16

Rapping with the "Boys" on the Street

The following dialogue came about when I had invited five local, unemployed young men (all in their mid-twenties), into my motor home which was parked opposite Clara's Sandwich Shop in Jelly Roll. Four of the five were already known to me as former employees at the mill. One had been fired when caught stealing from the company, another terminated after frequent absenteeism, and two others had quit or been discharged several times before because of drinking problems. I had had previous conversations with all of these men, sometimes casually on the street, on two occasions related to their rehabilitation for jobs, and at other times I had visited them at home. Three of the five were second generation employees at the mill.

These background remarks are intended to alert the reader to the fact that the free-wheeling, intimate dialogue which follows did not evolve among strangers. But of greater importance, all of these young men exemplify the strong voice of a dissenting counter culture towards the traditional values of the community. Theirs' is a minority report, forceful and significant, a life style and code of conduct sharply in contrast with the majority of their age peers who have married, formed households and hold regular jobs, successfully integrating themselves into the more traditional community.

Taking a break

Yeah, I guess you'd call us street people.

That's our handle.

These people around here gotta strong mind to blame you for everything that goes on.

Watch out! We've got a bad reputation. People think we're rough. [laughter]

If you think we're rough, you ought to meet up with some of these really young punks. Raised believin' nothin', never been punished, parents just keep feeding them while they're hollerin', 'I'm not gonna do this or that.'

None of 'em keep a job; walk off first time they don't like something.

They're bold. They're violent. Quick to do any damn fool thing. Not scared to cut on you.

Every generation is growing up faster than before.

That's the way of the world.

Well, how rough they gonna get?

Sounds like you're scared.

Not me.

Young people need a place to go, release pressure because the tracks is getting faster and faster.

They're all smokin' dope and screwin' when they're twelve or thirteen, for Christ's sake!

Calion's one of the few places where you can walk down the middle of the street with a beer and a joint and nobody will mess with you.

This street's an easy home, but it gets tiresome. I'd rather have a job I liked.

We've worked this street over. I con you today. You con me tomorrow. We've done everybody at one time or another. El Dorado is something else. You can always make a hustle, find a whore or a game there.

If we're lucky around here we can get high, stay high all day.

It's so dull. Lotsa times I go home at night, eat and go to bed by eight o'clock.

Well, why don't you get married? Then you can really be bored. [laughter]

How do you get married to a married woman? They're the ones I go for. But if they don't have a good job, I don't want them. She gives you a little somethin' and I give her a good screwin' and she appreciates it.

I wouldn't mind getting hitched if I found the right woman and made up my mind to it. She'd have to have a good job and I'd get one too. Split fifty-fifty. You can't make it now unless both of you are working.

In Calion you need to own your own crib. You need a

car to go to town, and you need money. Then you can do like you want with a girl on each arm.

You mean this broad today, that one tomorrow.

Let's face it, we're just sittin' here livin' for today, waitin' on the next drink, workin' on the next hustle. Admit it, nobody is thinkin' about tomorrow.

Tomorrow we get high again if we're lucky.

I hate the weekends if I got no money. Doesn't matter much during the week.

You mean when she says, 'Oh, Joe, buy me a beer' and you don't have a damn penny.

Sometimes you can rake a yard or hop a day on the garbage truck if you need a few bucks bad.

I'm busted and winter is coming. Then it's tough on the streets and no house parties.

Yeah, everybody gets dog-faced in winter.

Police cars don't prowl as much in winter. Fat asses stay by their heaters. Don't check things out. It's a safer time for a nice little ripoff.

The jails are full, this county and all over the state. They won't hardly put you away in winter. The judge don't want to feed you all winter long. [laughter]

They say that if they send you up now they got no room; let one out to let one in.

Winter brings a harder hustle but a safer one.

Nothin' beats pushin' dope [marijuana]. I can clear two hundred bucks while you're tryin' to peddle a couple of car batteries for twenty-five bucks.

And it will mellow you out while you're workin'.

Dope's a good hustle alright, but you got to watch your step.

There are rats in every hole!

Now don't you think we're hip? Real big-time hustlers!

Shit, I'd rather have a job.

We're hip man. Calion is hip. We're no bunch of country bumpkins. Girls are surprised with our rappin'.

When we go to El Dorado they respect us.

Prefer us over those El Dorado dudes.

When we walk into a bar they move over to make room for us.

We're tough and we stick together.

If one of us gets in a fight the rest will join in to polish off their ass.

Outsider hasn't got a chance against us.

If I had a truck, I would never need to go to work for the man. I could make it on yard jobs, hauling firewood and still go where I pleased, when I pleased.

Yard work, my ass, pushin' dope's the easy way. You must be crazy talkin' yardwork shit.

The good thing about the old folks here is if they like you they'll give you somethin' to do. Not much pay. Just enough to get you by.

It's nice to know everybody in town.

This is a good place to live.

Dull, but good. Go to town to get your kicks.

Give me fifty or a hundred bucks and I'll make my move, get cleaned up, dressed up — cool, calm and collected.

Last time I was up town duded out I met this sweet thing and she told be, 'My old man hasn't touched me in seven days.' I borrowed a pick-up truck and took her out a back road. We parked and I reached for it and she didn't have any pants on. God! she was hot, pantin' like a choo choo train. She was big and I was gettin' that way. We fumbled around in the truck for a while, then I stretched her out right there on the gravel road!

You're a hard lover, ain't you, Slim.

This tool won't work in no small places. [laughter]

Now nappy head here is havin' trouble gettin' it up, I hear.

Where you hear that bullshit?

That widow woman's tellin' on you.

Sometimes I'm not in the mood. It takes me while. But I'm a pro, I never disappoint them.

Listen at the man talk it up!

You know it. Now sometimes they can mess you up good. Right, Slim? Tell 'em about what Shirley did to you.

That big mama gave the worst case of clap [gonorrhea] I ever had. Took three shots to cure it up. Never said she was sorry.

Hell, when I was growin' up I kept a case of clap all the time.

You haven't gotten any good pussy till you got the clap. [laughter]

They just get the clap knocked out and up jumps this herpes stuff.

It's the shits, isn't it?

These women take a lot out of a man.

The competition's gettin' tough. You got to freak out [oral sex] on all these women now.

Your a real Pac man! [expert in oral sex].

You got to meet the competition on your knees, boy. This town's full of lesbians and they're after the same women you're after.

And they're workin' right down there in that furniture plant.

A dozen of them. [He calls out six or seven names.]

And that's not the half of 'em. Women old enough to be your grandmother, all lesbians. They're comin' out in the open more all the time. Walk out in the street arm in arm. Out hustlin' like us.

Get out here on a Saturday and watch 'em if you don't believe it.

Have you seen them work? A woman knows how to touch a woman just right. They know every spot. One little touch and they tremble with pleasure. A few strokes and they go wild.

If their mother's got it in her blood, the young ones got it in them, too.

They mostly go both ways. Take a man's money spend it on another dike.

It's not right the way these women do!

Shit, man, it's part of the action. We just have to be like Pac man here and meet the competition head on! [laughter]

What this town needs is more women. We know the ones here too well.

Come on, boys, today is Mother's Day. [First day of the month when welfare checks come out.]

Right on time. Today's the day we wine and dine.

Don't you bastards ever get tired of courtin' those women? I'm tired of these streets. Wish I was workin' at the mill. I messed myself up when I stole from the company. Pussy made me do it because it will make you do anything. Just give me a job now and I'll go home happy.

Whose got a dollar? I need a beer.

Are you going to put anything except your voice in the pot?

We don't need a beer, we need a case.

It'll take a case to oil up the sweet talk for our lady friends tonight. [laughter]

Women do loom large in the Jelly Roll community. This is a simple reality not to be distorted by overemphasis. It does not raise the specter of a pathological matriarchal society with all its proported flaws and weaknesses as proposed by Moynihan (1965). The importance of women here in Jelly Roll has neither mauled nor mutilated the male ego. The men at home and on the street seem robust enough. They have not been shamed into impotence, nor cowed into submission. Their macho attitudes and life style are very much in evidence; but despite this fact, women in Jelly Roll dominate the domestic scene. That is to say, in a significant majority of households, women allocate the money and pay all the bills, have access to the welfare system when necessary, supervise and discipline the children, grandchildren and sometimes other dependent adults, direct religious training and maintain contact with the schools.

However, contrary to comparable statistics for large black urban communties, the overwhelming majority of women in Jelly Roll (86% excluding elderly widows) have a husband or other live-in working male consort. This would suggest that the dominant role played by black women is not necessarily derived from nor dependent upon the absence of male bread winners. The usual stereotype of matriarchal households visited but little affected by temporary male consorts, who tend to be weak and emasculated by unemployment or meager wages, does not fit the full employment Jelly Roll community. Here, men are accustomed to bringing home the principal paycheck. It does not explain the dominant role played by women, nor does it provide a basis for the strong male macho cult with its attendant infidelities, hostility toward women, sexual competitiveness and deep-seated suspicion toward wives and lovers. Black macho may have been encouraged or even spawned by the historic suppression of black men. If so, we are dealing with a cultural remnant, a compensatory device from the past without present justification.

The entrenched cult of masculinity, so forcefully proclaimed by the street people in our interview, also mirrors the traditional commercial role of sex in black America, sex as a market commodity, bargained for and exchanged for money and favors, goods and services (Liebow 1967). For sex has always been an integral part of the historical solution to the black community's economic deprivation and suppression, to a cash-short society inhabited by the unemployed and underpaid. The precedent for the solution may go back to slavery, or for that matter, further back to African polygamy (Genovese 1976). Be that as it may, the tradition can no longer be supported in purely economic terms in Jelly Roll, where good wages and full employment prevail.

Romantic love, a universal American preoccupation, is a goal and cultural expectation in Jelly Roll also, but it floats remotely beyond the trysts and trafficking in sexuality. Therefore, because the sale of sex is often embellished with protestations of romantic love, there are forever feelings of tension, false motives and anticipated double dealing between the sexes.

Sexual competition in Jelly Roll is compounded by the "Female Conspiracy," the close world of cooperation and alliance between women. Obviously, this state of affairs preys upon the minds of the boys on the street and poses what they view as "competition" in their world. The relationships between women, while competitive as far as men and sexual favors are concerned, are characterized by close cooperative ties within the nuclear family and between generations of the extended family. From childhood, the mother-daughter relationship is bonded by the shared duties of housekeeping and the care of the younger children. Similarly, sisters close in age, relishing the role of little mother, will usually work harmoniously to cook, clean and care for younger siblings. As we have seen from several profiles, the older family household is frequently impacted by an unmarried or divorced daughter's return with her small children, sometimes to stay herself, but more often to leave one or more children with her own mother for extended periods or indefinitely. Even where a father or grandfather is present, it is a woman's world that greets the observer in these teeming multi-generational households. Older men are likely to oppose unsuccessfully and to resent the return of their daughters and their children. Mothers and daughters care for and discipline the children, pay the bills, take or send children to church and go to the school when there is trouble. Macho men, on the whole, bring home their paychecks or a part of it, gather on the streets, and more often than not pursue a clandestine affair with another woman and spend a limited amount of time at home, where they are likely to precipitate an argument over watching sports events or sit-coms on the single television set.

Unfortunately, this cult of the macho male lives on after marriage and continues to provide its own pathways to pleasure and accomplishment wherein the traditional masculine values of hunting, fishing and carousing with the boys are augmented, especially by the younger men, with the hustling life style and continued adventures as stud conquerors. The success of a marriage will often impinge on the ability and willingness of the husband to relinquish his macho ways and become domesticated, as a majority generally do in time, at least to some degree.

Contrary to Freudian expectations, despite a mother-centered upbringing, there are only two openly acknowledged homosexuals in Jelly Roll, although there are innuendoes and accusations, mostly made by women, that there are a number of bisexual "closet boys" about town. Nonetheless, since conclusive determination is beyond the competence of this study, the impression remains that male homosexuality is minimal here. Possibly it is suppressed by the omnipresence of the macho cult. On the other hand, there is much talk among the men, which is reluctantly confirmed by the women, about the increasing frequency and bold display of female homosexuality, a long-tabooed subject only recently scrutinzed in the behavioral sciences. Initially the suggestion that there might be a high incidence of lesbian contacts in this little rural community seemed both unexpected and improbable. Were not women, with few exceptions, forever involved in this society in a never-ending romantic struggle with the opposite sex? Indeed, women unattached to men to one degree or another are rare in this community. However, when considered more circumspectly, the practice of bisexual lesbianism as a "second calling" should not come as a surprise in such a provocative environment. In Jelly Roll male-female tensions and suspicions are the antithesis of female-female cooperation, intimacy and mutual protection. Women are more likely to share scarce resources, especially at the end of the month before welfare checks arrive, and when delinquent utility bills threaten interruption of vital services. They share long-term care of infants, socialization, schooling and religious life. In short, the junctures of intimacy between women are in sharp contrast with those shared with changing male partners in an atmosphere fettered by male machismo with its attendant suspicions of infidelity and double dealing.

Little wonder, then, that intimacies between women should sometimes culminate in homosexual love, and that the inferred increase in lesbian relationships in Jelly Roll may have occurred routinely in these permissive times where the latent is more likely to become openly manifest.

CHAPTER 17

Lovella Jones

Someday, Their Father Will Marry Me

Lovella is twenty-one years old and the mother of five children. Poor health and the lack of a family-supported network have kept her from applying for work at the mill. She lives alone in a dilapidated old frame house with broken steps and a leaky roof. The ceiling hangs loose precariously, the peeling wallpaper is brown with age and water marks, the furniture is worn and musty. The windows are boarded up and stuffed with paper to preserve precious heat. Even at midday, the house is in near total darkness, except for a single light bulb hanging in the middle of the living room. Lovella is a small, thin girl, but with a determined and optimistic air about her that denies everything that might appear to others as desperate poverty. With her year-old daughter slumped in a deep sleep in her lap, the television glaring out of the darkened back room where her other children sprawl on the floor, she begins her candid account from her early teenage years of what brought her to her present state:

> I first got pregnant at thirteen. Billy was a year older than me. He's been my only love. All my children are his. . . . But that first time I got pregnant, Mother grabbed me by the arm and took me off to a doctor in Little Rock for an abortion. I thought she was taking me for a check-up, and he did it to me before I knew what was going on. Mama and I had some kinda fight after that. I took an infection and

almost died. I'm still sick a lot, makes me lose time at work, which the bosses don't appreciate. The doctor says I might always have this infection because of that bad abortion. I really ought to sue, but that would involve my mother. . . .

Anyway, Billy got me pregnant again the next year. Mother was furious all over again. I had to run away. She got the police chasin' after me to bring me back home. There I was pregnant, runnin' through the back woods, jumpin' ditches trying to get away from the Law and Mama! I ended up leavin' home for good. Billy's family took me in, and that's where I had Billy, Jr. I was fifteen. . . .

I made the tenth grade before I had my next baby, Joe Pat. Things was too crowded at Billy's mama's house by then, so I rented this old house just around the corner, and I've been livin' here to this day. After Joe Pat was born, I had to go to work full time to support these kids. Now they are six, four, three, two and one. But I'm gettin' along pretty good on those birth control pills. I'd tried takin' them before, but they made me sick. . . .

I love 'em, but I've got enough kids. I've had a hard time with these kids of mine. Don't you know my mother has given me fits about them. She never liked Billy. All of my family have given me a hard time about Billy. Once I had to put an ice pick in my brother's arm when he got on my case. You see why I don't go home much? I can't go to Mother about nothin'. Grandma is something else. She's the one who cooked our good breakfast, pressed our hair and listened to our troubles. But I never forget Mother's Day, her birthday and Christmas. She'll sit my older kids when Billy and I go off to a church meeting sometimes. Mostly, Billy's mother takes care of the kids while I'm at work or at church. I get along wonderful with her. She had eighteen children of her own and seventeen are still living. She helps with the money, too, when she's able. Her husband has two jobs, but sometimes he goes off for weeks at a time; then things get scarce. Billy does the same thing. . . .

Would you believe it! I've been with Billy nine years this Fourth of July. No, it hasn't been easy. I'm blessed when I'm not behind on my bills and can pay some each week. Billy is going to school every day and only works a little part time at the poultry plant. Sometimes he takes a notion to help out and sometimes he doesn't. Right now he's in one of his wild moods. I may not see him for a while. I could wake up tomorrow and find him married to somebody else. I'm never sure. I don't tell anybody he's gonna marry me. If he leaves, he leaves. That's it. But I pray that someday we'll be married; it's a long struggle waitin' for that man of mine. . . .

> Sure, we've talked about marriage. Maybe when he gets out of college. Mama says when he graduates he'll probably marry somebody else, that's the way men do you. People don't understand me, but he's my man. I don't care what he does when he's not with me. When he's here stayin' with me, he's here. When he's out, he's out. After all, he's not my husband, is he? When he wants to come home to me, he'll come home to me. I'm not one of those girls who talk a man into getting married only to turn around and have a divorce be waitin' on them. If I get married, I want to be married till I die. We've gone for years without a fight until the marriage talk gets heavy.
>
> I've been in a long battle, and I'm still fightin'. Billy's getting his degree this August. He has a letter promising him a job in Little Rock as soon as he's out of school. No, I don't know whether he's takin' me and these kids with him. If he leaves them, it's him that's losin' them. If he leaves us, he leaves us, but one thing's for sure, I'm not stayin' here waitin' on him. I'm going to California to see my father probably or somewhere. I try to just take it as it comes, try not to get uptight in my mind about it. My pastor says he doesn't see how I put up with that man, but it's just the way I am, and nobody really understands me. . . . I've been saved and sanctified in the Blessed Savior Church. I go to church every night I can. I won't wear pants, don't drink or smoke. I've never been in a nightclub or honky tonk. My life is just workin' to raise these kids with the Lord's blessing.

Obviously Lovella Jones has been cruelly exploited by the worst sort of chauvinist macho male. Still, Lovella defends him against all accusations, whether they come from her mother, brothers, sisters, friends or pastor. Tough, independent and headstrong though she is, her dilemma derives from a tenacious romanticism and an almost medieval acceptance of male dominance and machismo. She is, moreover, an example in the extreme of one caught in the black female's painful and costly love affair with motherhood itself. For those young women for whom middle class opportunities do not knock or the challenge and odds seem too great to achieve higher goals in education, career or a good marriage, there is always the personal triumph of their sex and fertility to fall back upon. "All I have to offer the world is my womanhood" is still a cultural goal of last resort (Ladner 1971).

Although Lovella's circumstances may be repugnant to middle-class morality, and she is regarded as foolish by many even in her own community, nevertheless, one cannot comfortably stand on the curb and scorn this mother of five. She has remained true to one man. He is a student and only an occasional provider; but true also to the traditional work ethic, she has not sought nor received government aid except for food stamps to supplement the low-paying service industry jobs she has held. She is a stranger to the comtemporary pop culture of booze, drugs, loud music and honky tonks; she is deeply religious, at times prudish in her attitudes.

Lovella was raised in a large conservative and traditionalist family that was overshadowed by her patriarchal grandparent. To a fault, she has always unquestioningly accepted male dominance. From a church-going family, she has herself made religion her refuge, her solace in adversity, as well as the center of her limited social life. She is respectful and solicitous of her parents, at the same time living far from her father and often at odds with her mother. Basically, she has only deviated from traditionalist norms by embracing her contemporary society's easy acceptance of illegitimate motherhood. Eagerly, at thirteen she took a lover, blithely accepted the prospect of pregnancy and reacted violently to her mother's arranged abortion. Even at thirteen she felt cheated of motherhood and almost at once became pregnant again, bearing a child almost yearly thereafter. Her only confessed bitterness centers around her mother's rejection of her conduct. Alienated from her conservative family, she found refuge with her boyfriend's mother, whose life style more closely paralleled her own; and here, she has continued to find support and comfort during the eight years since she left home. Her long struggle at low wages in short-order restaurants in order to care almost single-handedly for her growing family has been only minimally successful, as her bare house and ragged children attest, an ordeal in payment for her love affair with a ne'er-do-well. In a sense, like a heroine in grand opera, her sin has been that she loved not wisely, but too well.

Stubbornly Lovella continues to justify and rationalize her demeaning life style and her frustrating relationship with Billy:

> What Mama and all of you don't understand is that there's never been anybody except Billy. Always Billy, nobody else. Do I still love him? [laughs] I guess I do, but it's not the same as it used to be. He comes, he goes. He sleeps in my bed when he wants. Right now, he's in another one of his crazy moods — got another woman. I never know when he's comin' around. But when he's not at school, especially on weekends, he'll lend me his car sometime and keep the kids while I go shoppin'. Not lately! Everybody tells me rumors that he's fixin' to get married to this other girl. Would you belive it! I read the wedding announcements in the newspaper everyday, hoping I won't see Billy's name. You think I'm crazy, don't you?
>
> Everybody gives me the same advice — get rid of him.

Get you another man. But, you know, it's hard to meet men. I won't go to bars and joints. Most of the men are already married. I met a nice older man at a church revival in Junction City. He talked real nice and I started likin' him some, but sure enough, he got around to admitting he was already married but says he's not gettin' on with his wife. You men! Where am I going to find a good man who wants me with all these kids?

Billy loves his kids. I think that's why he sticks around. His mama will sit them anytime unless they're bad sick. She be like a mother to me. I go by her house every night after work to pick up the baby. We have a visit and sometime she gives me somethin' to take back for our supper. And when my stamps come in, I take her things. Who else can I count on? My own mother won't keep my kids. Whenever I go to see her she gets all swelled up and there's always a fight. You've seen us together. Aren't we a mess? So I don't go, do I? I stays right here waitin' on Billy because that's just me.

Soon after this interview session, Lovella lost her most recent job as a short-order cook because health problems related to her abortion years ago often kept her from working. Her personal frailty, sick children, an old car that sometimes wouldn't start led inevitably to an unacceptable number of job absences, although she is clearly a good and conscientious worker. "A whirlwind in the kitchen with a very agreeable personality, she's a charmer," said one employer. Yet, all these positive attributes could only serve to hold her job a few more times after missed days, until inevitably each consecutive employer judged her charm and skill less important than her unreliability.

I usually don't get mad when they fire me. Some of them are very nice men. I know it's my fault. If you're hungry askin' for a hamburger, you don't want to hear about how the cook's car wouldn't crank. . . . I've worked 'em all. You can't name a hamburger joint in this town where I haven't worked [giggles]. I've worked the hospitals, too [in food service]. I liked that better. Maybe I can go to school and take nursing. I'd like to be able to say, 'Hey, I'm doin' somethin' for people instead of always needin' a favor. . . .

But what can I do? I need an operation. The doctor said I'd never be right, always on medicine until I have it. I've put in an application for Medicaid and been turned down. Who would pay the bills or take care of the kids while I'm in the hospital? Who's gonna take care of me? You see, I'm a person with lots of troubles. I'll bet I'm boring you. Are you sure I'm not?

> What I mean [laughs], I mean what I really need is to win one of those big quiz show prizes. Then I would have this operation, go back to work with a better car. I could keep the bosses happy and keep a job while I'm studying to be a nurse. The last of my kids will be in school next year. Maybe that will be my year to get it all together!

Unfortunately, Lovella ran out her employment string after her last dismissal. Her reputation on the fast food strip in El Dorado had finally caught up with her, and, despite her daily rounds to the restaurants, she secured no new job. Then, to add to her troubles, a severe cold spell without enough antifreeze in her car resulted in a cracked engine block. After that, the old car was not salvageable. Now broke and stranded without transportation, Lovella reluctantly turned, not to welfare, but to domestic service as employment of last resort. Through her mother's connections in El Dorado, she found two young mothers in need of part-time help. Here at least, she could deal with housewives who were more lenient and flexible in their work hours. As always, Lovella's winning personality and eagerness to work won over her new employers, who, although they held strictly to the low prevailing wage of twenty dollars a day, showered her with hand-me-down clothes for her children and herself. Access to good physicians was also quietly arranged. A used refrigerator was both donated and delivered to her house when her old unit failed.

Moreover, Lovella had not survived on her own these last nine years without acquiring much of the agility and guile of an accomplished con artist. Sometimes her employers' friends, whom she had often met only casually and briefly, nonetheless received urgent phone calls from "little Lovella" begging a modest loan with assurances of repayment in weekly installments from her wages. Sometimes the title to her car was offered as reassuring collateral or the promise to baby sit, work a party or provide other services were committed in advance, all to cover the continuing gap between earned income and unpaid bills. Lovella lives in a world of debts and accumulated needs. One of her children suffers from a chronic ear infection, another from asthma, and Lovella requires major surgery. The electrical appliances necessary to everyday life are without exception in disrepair and on the verge of breakdown. Her vintage car, with six monthly payments still due, is beyond salvaging. Stove, refrigerator and hot water tank are in various degrees of dilapidation. Actually, about ten thousand dollars in cash would be necessary to get Lovella, her children and home fixed up and caught up — shades of the quiz show windfall of which she dreams.

Probably the most disheartening fact of her situation is the realization that the day after this imagined windfall was used up that the cumulative process of falling behind would inevitably begin again, for none of her intrinsic financial problems would have been solved. Most pressing among Lovella's instant needs is a skilled occupation, such as that of a practical nurse, whereby she might become financially autonomous. Or, another solution would be a faithful husband with steady employment. However, here again, even for a very attractive young woman in this society, there is an obvious dearth of eligible and accessible mates. Almost every woman agrees. "The competition's rough, and women are paying for these 'sonny boys.'

Thus, Lovella seems fated to continue frantically treading water just to survive in dire poverty, only vaguely hopeful that she will be rescued by "her man," who appears neither willing nor able to come to her aid. Experience suggests that most women after some months, a year at most, would seek supportive relationships with other men even if they continue to cohabitate with their previous mate. However, Lovella, although stung by Billy's blatant philandering and lack of support, has been a poor adjuster when measured by the standards of her own culture. Her persistent antagonism to her mother has denied her the formidable support system employed by the poor for food, shelter, money and child care. Without this family support she has not been freed to work in the furniture plant where she could earn a living wage. Instead, she has relied upon a mother-in-law already burdened with many children of her own and whose erratic support and divided allegiances have made her a less than adequate substitute for Lovella's own family.

Compounding the weakness of her in-law support system, she has been denied more than token support from public welfare which has steadily penalized her for holding low-paying jobs. Passively Lovella has refrained from actively seeking another man to contribute to her family's needs; and many men near her own age, "Sonny Boys," usually expect to receive — not give — support. Lovella's mother urges her to "find an older man who will show you he appreciates you," an unromantic thought against which Lovella stands firm. Thus, the intrinsic commercial aspect of so many male-female relationships limits her prospects of finding another mate in her own age set. At twenty-two her youthful appeal is already slipping away. She is gaining weight. Soon her appeal to other men will be measured primarily by her income. Much of her social life is already spent with women in similar circumstances. Looking for "Mr. Right" has so often been influenced by the macho cult as to become an almost nonexistent ideal. And so Lovella waits and dreams because she finds no alternative to dreaming.

CHAPTER 18

Summary and Conclusions

The Paradoxes of Progress

After more than three years of continuous study in this neighborhood community, a candid summing up is in order. I make no pretense that I ever became an integral part of the community. However, I continue to assert the viability of a study such as this one in which I could maintain an involved detachment or objectivity, a vested, concerned role that could not forestall partisanship, but which did permit me the freedom to let the chips fall where they may. Unlike the passing relationships taken by most investigators in similar studies, I was and continue to be a trusted outsider, a friend of long standing with long-term commitments to this community. Even though I was sometimes misinformed, sometimes quietly refused sought-after information, sometimes exploited for small loans or favors, sometimes just grudgingly tolerated, in any case, my commitment to the community, and them to me, continues. It does not end with the writing of the last page of this book, for they and I are in Calion to stay. Jelly Roll continues to fascinate me, to draw me into its vortex at the end of my day at the mill. There are the same old ambivalences of admiration and disapproval, arousing a rush of conflicting emotions that seldom fail to accompany each visit. There is the same excitement of time spent with the porch sitters. Yet above all else, I have felt a growing respect for the toughness and resilience that characterize the people who live here and their good-humored tenacity in the face of trouble.

Now, in a very real sense, personal troubles are the moving force in this little neighborhood, troubles real and imagined, imposed from outside and self-inflicted from within. Historically, most of the peoples' troubles were derived from the burdens of economic exploitation, discrimination and poverty; but now once-successful adaptive strategies such as the use of sex to gain money or concessions, cohabitation out of wedlock and the cult of the macho male continue to disrupt black family life.

In Jelly Roll, as elsewhere, the dashing figure and the capers of the macho male continue to enjoy popularity as a role model for the young but in an atmosphere of growing criticism and resistance from the women of the community. As a positive example for male behavior, machismo has not lost its glamour nor been easily set aside, even in marriage, but rather continues to create tensions between husband and wife, to foment infidelities and generally to poison the relationship of natural affinity and cooperation between the sexes. Still, a majority of Jelly Roll matches that are cemented by marriage and economic success seem eventually to accommodate traditional middle-class monogamy. Even if we recognize that economic success is the single most important external factor in the stability and vitality of the black family (Billingsley 1968) and (Scanzoni 1971), then internally the tolerance of the macho cult is the source of its greatest peril. Male infidelity, often countered with female infidelity, is not only disruptive to the conjugal family but also expensive and, therefore, a drain upon limited resources. After the accusations of love's disillusionment, the long hard fights over money quickly follow; and a woman's first suspicions that her man is untrue come home with his first or second short pay check. While the reasons for any man's philandering are many, crossing boundaries of race or class, it is the tolerance of a whole gamut of attitudes and behavior encompassed by black machismo that particularly concerns us here (Wallace 1978).

Black machismo begins with a young man's immunity from responsibility for his sexual acts. The fact that young men are seldom taken to task for the seduction of even a very young virgin makes young girls the special object of their ambitions. Moreover, pregnancy is a predictable result of the affair where the macho male is contemptuous of birth control and the young girl considers her first child as no less than a triumph of womanhood (Ladner, 1971). Traditionally, there is little expectation of responsibility on the part of the father . Only too often the young male goes free, unencumbered by financial obligation, the obligation to marry or social repercussions, and therefore free to seduce and inseminate again. Frequently, but with noteworthy exceptions, the young mother, her parents and the government are left to cope with the pregnancy, offspring and all ensuing complications. Predictably, the children of the children are shunted back a generation to be raised by those who may have already had more of their own than they wanted or could afford.

So the cult of machismo begins by victimizing black society's most vulnerable nubile youth and continues throughout the life cycle, through a repetition of conquests, to ravage the economic, social and emotional roots of the black family. All too frequently a painful and disruptive transience comes to characterize the male-female estate.

In Jelly Roll a lack of male-female harmony is evident even where the economy should permit the black family to flourish. Symptoms of internal instability emerge in multigenerational households when the homes of older parents are impacted by returning daughters and their children fleeing disrupted conjugal relationships. Moreover, the presence of the macho cult also implies a reluctance to marry, a situation manifested in our community both by the high incidence of common-law relationships as well as the remarkably large number of bachelors of all ages.

The prevalence of multigenerational families should be perceived as part of the solution, certainly not as part of the problem. As the interviews clearly communicate, these extended families, especially through the women who play such a large role within them, provide a strong emotional and social support system for the children whom they harbor. The extended family institution, seldom available to the children of broken homes in comparable white society, is capable of raising the dynamic, self-confident personalities which appear repeatedly in our little community. Not social pathology but social vitality greets us in Jelly Roll!

The question that remains is how to mold the affective energies and strong personalities here into a more stable and emotionally efficient family unit.

Unfortunately, welfare subsidies for children have inadvertently reinforced the macho cult, although there have been recent attempts to identify and hold fathers accountable for child support. However, in circumstances of high male unemployment and undercover employment, these efforts can at best anticipate only meager success and may cause a backlash by driving men further away from female-centered households. Nationally, secure jobs at a living wage remain a distant goal for many men, and high unemployment only seems to reinforce the macho cult (Liebow 1967). As the relatively prosperous community of Jelly Roll has shown us, commensurate with economic success there needs to be nothing less than a cultural crusade to discredit and disenfranchise the cult of machismo. This is an awesome task that ultimately must enlist the conscious and coordinated support of every black community organization as well as the Social Services bureaucracy on a national scale.

To summarize this book is to look back on the changing character and culture of a black society that began in poverty and discrimination but was fortified by a powerful Christianity and biblical literature, as well as a practical ingenuity that knew how to make an art of the possible. Three Jelly Roll generations in profile have revealed a disturbing net loss of certain kinds of cultural content. Far more than just nostalgia for the good old days, there is a palpable, quantifiable loss of verbal skills and breadth of vocabulary, a loss of familiarity with much of their rich biblical literary heritage, and the loss of practical skills and knowledge, most noticeably in the domestic arts of food preparation, sewing, quilting, horticulture, animal husbandry, carpentry and even motor mechanics. All of these skills had provided a rich experiential mosaic that was incorporated into the vocabulary of everyday life. When these skills, along with the central focus of their lives in the church, were preempted by a cash and carry economy, a rapid atrophy of cultural content and experience occurred. In an ironic switch from economic to cultural privation, the black community has abandoned much of its cultural heritage and has eagerly squandered its hard-won economic prosperity on that which is trivial and shallow in contemporary mass culture.

Jelly Roll's blacks are zealous converts to the electronic media. Television is omnipresent in their lives. Only in the homes of the elderly does one occasionally find a darkened set at any waking hour of the day or night. Television's stimulus alternates between total rapt attention and a background continuum to which one can turn when conversation slackens or when an interpersonal encounter becomes awkward or tense. In this way, television acts as a social crutch for all to lean on in a semi-darkened room.

The conversations of adults as well as children are animated by frequent references to the soaps, sit-coms and sporting events that occupy their idle hours. Books other than the Bible are seldom in evidence; not even magazines are read extensively, for the spoken word and electronic media are the prevailing stimuli.

Nor does the bureaucratized mediocrity of the local public school system generate much enthusiasm for learning and the written word. In working-class Jelly Roll, few express pleasure in academics. Getting by is the name of the game, with English and math as real stumbling blocks to graduation for many. What enthusiasm there is for the educational experience here revolves around sports events, parades and field trips, parallel phenomena to the electronic media.

The younger generation of church goers has also come to rely heavily upon the spoken word as the primary stimulus for faith. Pastors long familiar with the art of oration preach to a whole new generation only vaguely familiar with Biblical language and content. They face a young congregation that lacks both the will and the concentration to handle lengthy sermons and readings from scripture. Even regular church goers profess much difficulty with the assimilation of exotic Biblical names, places and language. Consequently, there is a trend in many, though not all, churches to revert to emotive rather than teaching styles, and hence the revival of the primitive churches that rely on the "stompin' and hollerin'" brand of religion to the exclusion of all else.

At the very heart of this black community's deculturation experience is the declining authority of the church. As late as the 1960s, the church's power base waxed strong as the catapult of their civil rights movement and the hub of black activism in the Christian community. At this stage and in this role, the politicized church continued to embrace its many followers in the larger sphere of scriptural literature, language and philosophy. Black Christian life and thought were thereby infused with an urgent vitality at the very time when religion was atrophying in white America. Only after the crusading phase of the civil rights movement had passed did the black church succumb to the inroads of prosperity and experience the inattentiveness of a restless younger generation accustomed to the quick fix of television. The young belong to an age who no longer identify with the children of Israel or the Messianic Jesus, whose humble sermon on the mount was the centerpiece of their parents' and grandparents' spiritual philosophy.

Nonetheless, we should not fail to look at the positive side of the mass media's blanket polarization, especially the media's role as urbane instructor to a remote rural community like Jelly Roll, where TV has brought a broader cognizance of the larger world. The young, in particular, have acquired from the media a wide-ranging world view that knows at least a little bit about a lot of things. Their Star Wars horizons have programmed them to accept more flexible or innovative solutions to the challenges of the present. They have added to an inherited resilience of spirit a boldness that is, at times, rash but which makes them willing candidates for more creative forms of training: in school, on the job or in the Army.

The media have helped arm the young and old alike with the

expertise to confront and manipulate the state and federal bureaucracies that impinge on their personal well-being. In Jelly Roll a great deal of emphasis is placed on knowing the ropes in accessing the welfare system; i.e., how to apply for various help programs, what to declare and what to hide, knowing one's rights and where to find a "good" lawyer that works on a percentage without a retainer.

As we have seen in our little community, welfare is pervasive. Yet, within this working class society, welfare retains the stigma of "easy money." Its recipients are widely gossiped about, with suspicion and sometimes envy, by their neighbors, the haves and have-nots alike. At best, welfare is a salvation to the old, the ill, the disabled, the incompetent and the dispossessed. At worst, it has made the able-bodied commit themselves to a demeaning life of idleness, a life that obliges recipients calculatingly or passively to avoid the workplace and thus forego any prospects for achievement, worker camaraderie and potential advancement. Choosing the welfare route leaves one beholden to administrators and bureaucrats of every persuasion. Welfare recipients have often greeted me with sheaves of papers to be deciphered and completed, for accepting welfare requires never-ending trips to the office "to keep your case straight." Periodic re-evaluations, reductions, cut-offs and oversights can strike fear and render real privation upon even the hardiest of families.

Moreover, welfare can become a tender trap for young unwed mothers who live technically on an illegal basis with a working or hustling man, enjoying the false reassurances of their comfortable combined income. In Jelly Roll, this temporary male consort typically has a late-model car and grosses $250 per week or more at the mill. When this income is added to a welfare mother's cash allotments, food stamps and Medicaid coverage, the couple enjoys the near equivalent of American middle-class affluence. Unfortunately, as we have repeatedly seen, such arrangements tend to be short-lived. There are seldom more than a few years before the welfare mother is jilted and abandoned to the competitive "meat market" or throws out an unproductive consort to seek another mate once more. Each time this occurs she is older, ostensibly less desirable, frequently with more children in tow; and, like Ruby Johnson, suffers an increased disadvantage in the competition with other women. Because sex is perceived as a commodity of exchange, male-female bonds tend to be weak without a marriage contract and commitment; but because of welfare regulations, marriage in turn, is often an economic disaster for the welfare recipient. All of this is a widely reported national phenomenon and is scarcely news (Gilder 1981). What is significant is that this obvious dilemma continues to be shrugged off by both those who administer and those who legislate welfare policy.

The pervasiveness of welfare, even in the good economic environs of Calion, can seldom be attributed to any laxity or lack of vigilance on the part of the Social Security bureaucracy. Rather, welfare's growth and abuse is directly related to the structure of the system itself, a veritable Swiss cheese of unadministrable and unenforceable rules and regulations wherein the adept find ample room to maneuver and manipulate (Gell 1969). Moreover, in recent years blacks have begun to approach welfare in the same opportunistic spirit in which the tax lawyers administer to America's upper classes. Fair game is fair game. For this country's black minority, long denied access to better paying jobs, welfare was originally perceived as a tithe on the white man's conscience, a gesture of reparations for past wrongs. The sentiment is often expressed in Jelly Roll that welfare is neither wrong nor bad, just unfairly distributed and often demeaning to obtain. In like manner until recently, the opposite was true among Calion's whites: welfare was wrong to exist in the first place and shameful to take, even when in need. As long as welfare was primarily a reparation provided to a few, the cost remained modest; but as it becomes an acceptable panacea to both blacks and whites, it also has become an accelerating burden on the public purse.

Jelly Roll is far from being a microcosm of black America. As a little community it is free from much of the terrible trauma and the demeaning life styles that characterize America's black ghettos. Nonetheless, this community may well demonstrate the pitfalls of transition that, even under benign conditions, working-class blacks must face in achieving equality in American society and culture. Along with the many inappropriate responses that are the heritage of this younger generation of blacks there is, on the positive side, a stalwart tradition nurtured in the extended family to endure hardships and to maintain a cheerful resilience in times of trouble. These traits give black character a unique strength and vigor. Black women offer forceful examples of how to survive with determination and humor in a hostile world. Lovella Jones, in the last chapter, is a captive victim of her culture, yet she acknowledges no enemy that cannot be vanquished through sheer will and persistence.

Many strong men live in Jelly Roll, but with few exceptions they are traditionally less verbal and animated than the women. Hard work and endurance have been their heritage in this rural setting; and old timers like Willie Cole and Deacon Clark bestow dignity and honor upon their modest role in working class America.

The deculturation, so lamented by Jelly Roll's oldsters, is part of the overall American dilemma of mass society and culture, an advanced case of the compounded afflictions of our modern world, tribulations unique only in the degree to which Jelly Roll has suffered cultural loss or the trauma associated with the problems of family disorganization. As a neighborhood community, Jelly Roll is an intensely personal place — full of joy, full of pain, fulsome in its expression of the human spirit, free from much of the private loneliness that so often haunts suburban America, blessed with an exuberant spirit that all may yearn to possess.

Bibliography

Anderson, Martin. *Welfare: The Political Economy of Welfare Reform in the United States.* Stanford, California: Hoover Institution Press, 1978.

Angelou, Maya. *I Know Why the Caged Bird Sings.* New York: Random House, 1970.

Bass, Barbara Ann, Gail Elizabeth Wyatt, and Gloria Johnson Powell. *The Afro-American Family: Assessment, Treatment and Research Issues.* New York: Grune & Stratton, 1982.

Bennett, John W. *Hutterian Brethren.* Stanford, California: Stanford University Press, 1967.

____________. *Northern Plainsmen: Adaptive Strategies and Agrarian Life.* Chicago: Aldine Publishing Co., 1969.

Billingsley, Andrew. *Black Families in White America.* Englewood Cliffs, New Jersey: Prentice-Hall, 1968.

Census of Population and Housing, Supplementary Report. Advanced Estimates of Social, Economic and Housing Characteristics. Arkansas: 1980.

____________. Supplementary Report. Summary Characteristics for Government Units and Standard Metropolitan Statistical Areas. Arkansas: U.S. Dept. of Commerce, 1983.

Dollard, John. *Caste and Class in a Southern Town.* New York: Doubleday, 1937.

Frazier, E. Franklin. *The Negro Church in America.* Shocken, New York: 1964.

____________. *The Negro Family in the United States.* Chicago: University of Chicago Press, 1939.

Gell, Frank. *The Black Badge: Confessions of a Case Worker.* New York: Harper & Row, 1969.

Genovese, Eugene D. *Roll, Jordan, Roll: the World the Slave Made.* New York: Random House, 1976.

Gilder, George. *Wealth and Poverty.* New York: Basic Books, 1981.

Glasgow, Douglas C. *The Black Underclass.* San Fransisco: Jossey-Bass Publ., 1980.

Glazer, Nathan and Daniel P. Moynihan. *Beyond the Melting Pot.* Cambridge, Mass.: M.I.T. Press, 1963.

Hall, Janice E. *Black Children: Their Roots, Culture and Learning Styles.* Provo, Utah: Brigham Young University Press, 1982.

Heiss, Jerold. *The Case of the Black Family: a Sociological Inquiry.* New York: Columbia University Press, 1975.

Jeffers, Camille. *Living Poor: a Participant Observer Study of Priorities and Choices.* Ann Arbor, Mich.: Ann Arbor Publ., 1967.

Jones, Reginald L. *Black Psychology.* New York: Harper & Row, 1972.
Karlan, Arno. *Sexuality and Homosexuality: A New View.* New York: W.W. Norton, 1971.
Kochman, Thomas. *Black and White Styles in Conflict.* Chicago: University of Chicago Press, 1981.
_____________. *Rappin' and Stylin' Out: Communication in Urban Black America.* Urbana, Illinois: University of Illinois Press, 1972.
Ladner, Joyce Ann. *Tomorrow's Tomorrow.* Garden City, New Jersey: Doubleday, 1971.
Lewis, Oscar. *Five Families: Mexican Case Studies in the Culture of Poverty.* New York: Basic Books, 1959.
_____________. *The Children of Sanchez.* New York: Random House, 1961.
Liewbow, Elliot. *Tally's Corner: a Study of Negro Streetcorner Men.* Boston: Little Brown, 1967.
Matusow, Allen J. *The Unraveling of America: A History of Liberalism in the 1960s.* New York: Harper & Row, 1984.
Moynihan, Daniel P. "Employment, Income and the Ordeal of the Negro Family," *Daedalus* 94, (Fall, 1965): 745-770.
_____________. Paul Barton, and Ellen Broderick. *The Negro Family: The Case for National Action.* Washington, D.C.: U.S. Dept. of Labor, 1965.
Myers, Lena Wright. *Black Women: Do They Cope Better?* Englewood Cliffs, New Jersey: Prentice-Hall, 1980.
Rainwater, Lee. *Behind Ghetto Walls: Black Families in a Federal Slum.* Chicago: Aldine Publ., 1970.
Redfield, Robert. *The Little Community: Viewpoints for the Study of a Human Whole.* Chicago: University of Chicago Press, 1955.
Roberts, J.R. *Black Lesbians: An Annotated Bibliography.* Tallahassee, Florida: Naiad Press, 1981.
Ryan, William. *Blaming the Victim.* New York: Random House, 1971.
Scanzoni, John H. *The Black Family in Modern Society.* Chicago: University of Chicago Press, 1971.
Schulz, David A. *Coming Up Black: Patterns of Ghetto Socialization.* Englewood Cliffs, New Jersey: Prentice-Hall, 1969.
Shimkin, D.B., Edith M. Shimkin, D.A. Frates, eds. *The Extended Family in Black Society.* The Hague: Mouton Publishers, 1978.
Stack, Carol B. *All Our Kin: Strategies for Survival in a Black Community.* New York: Harper & Row, 1974.
Staples, Robert. *The Black Woman in America: Sex, Marriage, and Family.* New York: Nelson-Hall, 1973.

Valentine, Betty Lou. *Hustling and Other Hard Work: Life Styles in the Ghetto.* New York: The Free Press, 1978.
Valentine, Charles A. *Culture and Poverty: Critique & Counter-proposals.* Chicago: University of Chicago Press, 1968.
Wallace, Michelle. *Black Macho and the Myth of the Super-Woman.* New York: Dial Press, 1969.
Warren, Donald I. *Black Neighborhoods.* Ann Arbor, Michigan: University of Michigan Press, 1975.
Washington, Joseph R. *Black Religion: the Negro and Christianity in the United States.* New York: Beacon Press, 1964.
Williams, Melvin D. *On the Street Where I Lived.* New York: Holt, Rinehart, and Winston, 1981.
Willie, Charles Vert. *A New Look at Black Families.* Bayside, New York: General Hall, Inc., 1976.

Appendix A

A Schematic Inventory of Jelly Roll Households
(With approximate ages of residents)

Nineteen Residences of Retirees: (Age 62 and older)

1. Widow, alone [Chapter 4 - Hattie Jenkins](1)
2. Widow, alone [Chapter 7 - Odelia Jackson](1)
3. Widower, alone (1)
4. Bachelor, alone (1)
5. Widower, alone (1)
6. Husband, wife and their (45) son (3)
7. Widow and her (40) son (2)
8. Husband and wife (2)
9. Widow and her (55) son (2)
10. Husband and wife [Ch. 6 - Erma & Jefferson Bates] (2)
11. Husband, wife, two (14, 16) daughters (4)
12. Husband, wife and her (35) son (3)
13. Widower, alone (1)
14. Widow, alone (1)
15. Spinster, alone (1)
16. Widow, alone (1)
17. Widow, two nephews (3)
18. Husband, wife (2)
19. Widow, alone (1)

Sixteen Extended Family Residences: (Three and four generations and/or grandparents with grandchildren)

1. Husband, wife (50s), wife's brother and his daughter (4)
2. Husband, wife (40s), four children (12-21), one grandchild (7)
3. Husband, wife (70s), two grandsons (20s) [Chapter 3 - Sylvester Malone] (4)
4. Husband, wife (50s), two children (20s), two grandchildren (6)
5. Widow (70s), daughter (40s), four grandchildren (8-19), two great-grandchildren [Chapter 9 - Ruby Johnson] (8)
6. Husband (50s), wife (40s), three children (12-15), one grandchild (6)
7. Husband, wife (60s), her grandson (10), his nephew (25) (4)

8. Widow (70), daughter (45), granddaughter (25), two great-grandchildren (5)
9. Husband, wife (40s), three children (8-17), one grandchild (6)
10. Widow (55), daughter (20), son (19), three grandchildren (6)
11. Husband, wife (60s), three children (20s), five grandchildren [Chapter 8 - Deacon Clark] (9)
12. Husband, wife (30s), five children (6-15), two grandchildren (9)
13. Husband, wife (40s), five children (6-15), two grandchildren [Chapter 10 - Leroy & Rose McCoy] (10)
14. Husband (60s), wife (55), two grandchildren (10, 15) [Chapter 5 - Willie & Babe Cole] (4)
15. Husband (30), wife (35), her three children (15-25), one nephew (15), one daughter-in-law (7)
16. Widow (60s), daughter (35), three grandchildren (7-16) [Chapter 14 - Erma Jean] (5)

Twenty-five (25) Residences - Married Couples: (Below age 62, alone or with their children only, including common law, two years or more)

1. Husband (30), wife (20s), one (5) daughter [Chapter 12 - Elmo & Angela Sanders] (3)
2. Husband, wife (20s), one (1) daughter (3)
3. Husband, wife (40s), three (10-18) children(5)
4. Husband (50), wife (40s), no children at home (2)
5. Husband, wife (50s) (2)
6. Husband (60), wife (55) (2)
7. Husband, wife (40s), four (11-22) children [Chapter 12 - Tommy & Mable Plunkett) (6)
8. Husband, wife (40), two (10, 12) children (4)
9. Husband, wife (40s), one ( ) daughter at home (3)
10. Husband, wife (20s), three (4-9) children [Chapter 12 - Henry & Donna Walters] (5)
11. Husband, wife (40s) (2)
12. Husband, wife (30s), five children (8-14) [Chapter 11 - Saphire and Wilbur Hines] (7)

13. Husband (50), wife (40), three (13-18) children [Chapter 12 - Randall & Mae Jefferson] (5)
14. Husband, wife (20s) (2)
15. Husband, wife (20s) [Chapter 13 - Evelyn & Mike Oliver] (2)
16. Husband, wife (20s), five (2-8) children [Chapter 17 - Lovella Jones] (7)
17. Husband (45), wife (40), her (20) son (3)
18. Husband, wife (20s), their (1) daughter (3)
19. Husband, wife (30s), two (6, 8) children (4)
20. Husband, wife (30s), four (8-13) children (6)
21. Husband (30), wife (20), one (1) child (3)
22. Husband (60), wife (60) (2)
23. Husband (55), wife (50) (2)
24. Husband (35), wife (30) (2)
25. Husband (30), wife (25), her two children, his two children (6)

Twenty Male-Headed Households: (With or without temporary consorts of less than two years)

1. Man, woman (20s), and her son (3)
2. Man (40), woman (30) (2)
3. Man (55), woman (45) (2)
4. Man (30), woman (30), and her five children (7)
5. Man (25), woman (20), and her daughter (3)
6. Man (30), woman (25), and her two children (4)
7. Man (25), woman (20) and her child (3)
8. Man (25), woman (25) (2)
9. Man (25), woman (20) (2)
10. Man (50) (1)
11. Man (55) (1)
12. Man (25), man (27) - brothers (2)
13. Man (60) (1)
14. Man (60) - Widower (1)
15. Man (32) [Chapter 14 - George Wesley] (1)
16. Man (40), separated, with two sons (18, 19)(3)
17. Man (25), divorced (1)
18. Man (30), divorced (1)
19. Man (28) [Chapter 14 - Moe Munson] (1)
20. Man (55) (1)

Four Female-Headed Households: (With or without temporary consort, less than two years)

1. Woman (25), divorced [Chapter 14 - Lenora Coleman]	(1)
2. Woman (50)	(1)
3. Woman (50), man (30)	(2)
4. Woman (20), man (30)	(2)

EPILOGUE

"I Thought I'd Be Free, But I Wasn't"

The black community of Calion, Arkansas, is on the move. Since *Jelly Roll: A Black Neighborhood in a Southern Mill Town* was published in 1986, many of the growing middle class have broken the historic bonds of manual labor and fled this "frog pond town," while those who have chosen to remain at the mill have gotten better-paying and more highly skilled jobs. However, between the high road to college and beyond and the old road to the mill lies a slippery slope called "the street"—sometimes perceived as a third career pathway.

The "street people" are a mixed lot. Their numbers include a hardcore of unemployed regulars, who, for a variety of reasons, do not seek conventional jobs. Others are wayfarers from many paths and places: relaxed retirees both old and young, drop-outs and drop-ins, hustlers, ex-cons, preachers without congregations, and casual visitors such as me, all welcome in a democratic spirit of good will. I have chosen to write about this group because their free-wheeling conversations so candidly convey strong opinions and attitudes about vital interracial and cultural issues.

During noon breaks at Calion Lumber Company (CLC), I enjoy stopping from time to time for a visit with this group of men sometimes referred to as the street people. This varied congregation of black males—women rarely attend—is located in a vacant lot on Mill Street with plenty of shade trees for protection from summer's intense sun. Situated on the primary road to the mill, this is the perfect spot to see and be seen, to gossip and transact, or simply to while away the day. Outsiders might describe such a day as idle or carefree, a simplified judgment at best. I have learned here that urgent needs often underlie the casual setting. I regard my time with this group as the antithesis of my own routine and a time for fellowship in an alternative lifestyle rich in humor and straight talk. Slim Jones, single, in his mid-forties, is a wit, an outspoken regular in what he refers to as the "no time clock for us club," an inclusive group of old and young, some that "get a check"—Social Security, etc.—as well as "dealers" and "players." Slim puts it this way:

> There's all kinds of workin', all kinds of hustle. Sweat work doesn't pay good because it's the easiest! Safes is the All-American way, right? . . . We all know dealin' drugs is the hardest work: up all night; push, push, push; then twin' to get some sleep between the phone calls during the day. Twenty-four/seven with no holidays—except time off for good behavior (in the jail house) Ha! Ha!

Slim, whom I have known since he was a boy, is one of the children raised in a stable family household. His father, Isaiah Jones, was a highly respected community leader both in his church and the company labor union. Most of his children completed high school or went beyond to acquire "responsible jobs" and successful lifestyles. But Slim was different. While inheriting his father's sharp intellect and ironic wit, he was aware of—and sometimes despairing of—his own lack of the self-discipline his father had personified. "I got no stick-to-it-ness," he would often lament as alcohol and every other available self-indulgence held sway in his life. Attempts to reform, to make a new start, have punctuated his career. But despite the encouragement of preachers, family, and other well-wishers, he inevitably "took a slide" back "into the arms of King Whiskey." Even after a most promising job interlude, he would fall away from work, and, depressed but relieved, he would holler to his friends, "Hey, I'm back!" When initial joy led to more solemn introspection, he would declare, "I hate it, but work makes me feel like I'm cheatin' myself."

Street people take pride in "straight talk," give no quarter, and offer few third-party excuses. Though they blame the dominant white culture for inadequate support, preparation, and sometimes blatant discrimination, they seldom dwell upon the outside forces that have so often confined their lives. Rather, they dote upon the very personal aspects of human motivation: "Now you know Ricky wants to be bad, but he don't have the guts. So what do he do? Has to work his ass off for CLC, ha, ha!". . . or this from an angry but concerned mother:

> I told Wanda, "You're too stupid to stay in school, too lazy to work regular, can't cook for a husband, won't pick up a wrap-

> per off the floor, but you sure like sex! So, honey, go ahead and be a whore, which you is! And if you're gonna be a whore, try to be a good one!"

It would appear that the great American work ethic knows no bounds! The rural South has traditionally left poor bequests to those blacks with abbreviated educations, little financial support, limited success, and historic prejudice. As a result, "alternative occupations" and lifestyles are ardently defended on the street as practical, rational forms of coping behavior—"making it" in an unfair society. In this regard, some lessons hit close to home.

Albert, a high-profile street man who was often in and out of jail, once explained to me why he had broken into our company cabin on Calion Lake. He assured me he had been careful not to damage the sliding aluminum door because once bent they were "hell to fix." Theft without unnecessary destruction—or remorse—was the rule:

> Now, don't take it personal, C.T.! Like in the movie I saw about this dude huntin' in Africa, the hunter showed respect for the animal he hunted. But he gotta do what he gotta do! Because he's in the jungle, right? In the movie he's leanin' over this rhino he just shot, and he's real sad you can—see a tear in his eye!

Crime against the white establishment is often perceived as "just gettin' even," sometimes as appropriate reparations for lost wars. "I'm Robin in the Hood, and I'm—punchin' my clock after dark!" Others, however, disagree:

> Robin Hoods? Be serious! Those cats aren't serious! They keep what they take. Some prey on their awn people. Why? Because they're so handy, like old ladies with hidden money just next door.

The predominant view of the street people is that "slave days" are over, but that equality has not arrived, that the dominant white society is still in charge. Anger and resentment in this black community may be diminished, but not dispelled. "Us versus them" is still the common vernacular. In the words of a high-profile street speaker,

> Modern times! Well, we got shiny new faces, don't we! But mine will always be black, and yours is everybody but us. Get it? Like what a fast talkin' white politician said down here the other day, "We're all equal now before the law." But what's that there behind the law? Whose white booties is hidin' back there? (laughter) The deck is still stacked, you hear me?

In the little town of Calion, as in much of the South, blacks and white freely intermingle on the job and in the town, but their respective cultures are often antagonistic, reflecting sharp differences in values and goals, despite regular exchanges at work, at school, on the playing field, at city hall, and at the local store. But only occasionally are more socially proactive gatherings integrated, such as barbeques, church services, and hunting clubs. Tellingly, intermarriage, the centerpiece of abiding integration, is still infrequent and receives uneasy, if not cynical, comment from both sides of the blanket: "So, Sammy went and got himself a Snow White skinny girl with—no job, no check, and two kids. She thinks the stove is just to warm up the Kentucky Fried chicken! Won't last— they'll break up when the strange is gone!" Or this: "Vicky loves her white boy, don't she? What's she see in him that I don't see? Her momma is prayin' he'll just fly away, ha! ha!" The chemistry of interracial accommodations proceeds here at its own slow pace.

Meanwhile, Calion's growing black middle class, energized by improved job opportunities, has embraced higher education as the vehicle for its growing aspirations. Therefore, going off to college when successful usually means leaving Calion forever for a new urban life. Those that remain behind are, nonetheless, heirs to a long, respected tradition of blue-collar labor. In the past sawmilling offered only hard, often hot, and always dangerous work where high-speed saws whirred with limited protection. The black men who manned these precarious work stations did so with mixed emotions: anger at the white owners and bosses whom they perceived as having minimal concern for their safety and well-being and keeping the best jobs for themselves, but also a strong sense of pride in coping with a dangerous occupation.

Today, with an OSHA-dictated safer workplace, traditional respect for manual labor remains strong but is qualified by better alternatives in this now upwardly mobile community. "Son, you goin' off to college, or are you goin' to CLC University? So, you're gonna work at the mill and get your letter sweater with the bird on it, ha, ha!" or this, "Man, it ain't so bad workin' here except I already know all the girls in this town," or "Baby, if you can't make it at CLC, you can't make it anywhere!"

Under the old shade tree on Mill Street one day flows effortlessly into another. The easy camaraderie, the blunt, bright exchanges rise and fall with the passing parade of visitors. The group remains open—tolerant even of outsiders like me, but sometimes with a warning:

> Hey, man, come on back anytime. We'll all be steady here. Yeah, some of us may be hustlin', and some may be buyin', but what's bein' given away that's what holds them here! And don't you forget it! Don't you go preachin' against us like you white boys don't want none of what we got, you hear me?—

The opening profile in Jelly Roll featured an eloquent speaker: Silvester Malone (real name is Gaddy Smith, deceased), who retired as a fireman in the Calion Sawmill boiler room. A fragment from a circa 1999 interview with him after the old sawmill was shut down is a fitting close to our mutual endeavors:

> "They told me my grandparents were slaves right here in Arkansas, but! don't know, I don't know. Anyhow, we were a captured race . . . still are . . . well. [In the past] we raised cotton on Champagnolly Hill. That's what made me strong. Couldn't stood that boiler room of yours 'cept I'd been raised a nigger on a white man's farm . . . I got white blood in me, too . . . who don't? Whites took what they wanted and—they wanted black girls [while] helpin' their mammas in the kitchen . . . justice! White man's justice all one sided. Their way the only way. I went to work at the mill thought I'd be free but I wasn't . . . , not till the end."